BUILT TO PROSPER FINANCIALLY

Wealth Is Your Birthright...
Build Yours

Hasheem Francis & Deborah Francis

Built To Prosper Financially: Wealth Is Your Birthright...Build Yours
Authors: Hasheem Francis & Deborah Francis
Cover design by: BTP Marketing Consultants
Edited by: Spirit of Excellence Writing & Editing Services, LLC
ISBN: 0615989314
Published by: BTP Publishing Group. Plymouth, FL **(www.BTPPublish.com)**

Books by Hasheem Francis & Deborah Francis

Built To Prosper

Built To Prosper For Women

Built To Prosper Financially

Built To Prosper Women of Wisdom Journal

Built To Prosper Wealth of Wisdom Journal

The Joy of Healthy Living; The Guide To Eating Right For Life

Cashology The Science of Living a Cash Only Life

Cashology Academy Wealth Workbook

Cashology Academy Wealth Journal

Undeniable Confidence

The Power of Effective Communication

The Science of Getting Rich: The Key To Peace, Power, & Prosperity

Seminars by Hasheem Francis & Deborah Francis

Built To Prosper For Life Seminars

Cashology Academy

The Joy of Healthy Living

Loyal Leaders Conference

Emerging Business Boot Camp

Young Entrepreneurs Academy

"Be a great student of life, so you can be an outstanding teacher of living." **Hasheem Francis**

Mentors Help YOU Excel To The Next Level! It is a fact that most people who mentor do it because they LOVE helping others! They love working with someone and helping him get from where he is to where he wants to be, bringing out his best, helping him think bigger, fostering those big breakthroughs, etc.

Built To Prosper Mentoring Program remains the most comprehensive program of its kind and a leader's best choice for exceeding his maximum goals. If you are highly motivated and want the individualized or corporate mentoring by one of our true experts, then you need our mentoring program. Our mentors specialize in giving you the latest techniques on how to build a profitable business, become an effective leader, amass wealth, and develop a healthy lifestyle. Your mentor will also instruct you on the most effective use of our proprietary materials and techniques. Built To Prosper Mentoring focuses on four areas: Business, Leadership, Wealth, and Health. Mentoring enables you to reach your full potential in life and gives you the ability to promote your personal and professional development in a strategic and supportive way, leading to enhanced returns on your investment.

Visit us at: www.BTPMentoring.com

DEDICATION

This book is dedicated to all who have the burning desire to study and apply the Built To Prosper principles and pass this wisdom on from one generation to the next.

- Hasheem Francis & Deborah Francis

DISCLAIMER

The information contained in this book is for informational purposes only.

Built To Prosper University does not hold itself out as providing any legal, financial or other advice. Built To Prosper University also does not make any recommendation or endorsement as to any investment, advisor or other service or product, or to any material submitted by third parties or linked to this material.

In addition, Built To Prosper University does not offer any advice regarding the nature, potential value or suitability of any particular investment, security or investment strategy.

The products and services mentioned in this book may not be suitable for you. If you have any doubts, you should contact an independent financial advisor. In particular, some of the investments mentioned may not be regulated under the Financial Services Act 1986 or at all, and the protection provided to you under this Act will not apply.

We make financial suggestions and it is up to you to make your own decisions or to consult with a registered investment advisor when evaluating the information of Built To Prosper University.

CONTENTS

RICH GLOBAL DIGITAL
CONCEPT
GOLD IDEA CHART CASH
ECONOMY
FASHION
INVESTMENT
LUXURY
FINANCE
ONE SIGN
LOSS FORECAST
SAVINGS
BANKNOTE CURRENCY
COIN
GAIN
TAX
EARNINGS GOAL
WEALTH
EURO
DOLLAR
BILLS
GOLD
CHART
SAVE
CASUAL
PROFIT
GRAPH
BUSINESS
SHINY
PLAN
MANAGEMENT
BUSINESSMAN
WOMEN
DEBT
CASH
CLOSE
DATA
PRICE
CALCULATION
FINANCIAL
GROWTH
CRASH
SHARES
RICH
SIGN
IDEA
COIN
FUND
NOBODY
MONETARY
CURRENCY
MARKET
BANK
BUSINESS
MONEY
CRISIS
PEOPLE
ART
SUCCESS
TREASURE
SYMBOL EXCHANGE
CREDIT
COMPANY
CAPITAL
HUNDRED
CONCEPTS
GOLDEN
ACCOUNTING
SALE
FORTUNE
PROSPERITY

INTRODUCTION

We would like to commend you for your commitment to investing in yourself. Financial literacy is the key to financial freedom. You should be proud of yourself for the excellent decision you've made to become a wealth builder. You have made an important decision to pursue financial knowledge, a decision that could ultimately result in unimagined and unlimited personal success. As you study this book, you will be embarking on a new and exciting chapter in your life. **Our mission is to teach One Million Families to become an example to their community of how powerful it is to be a wealth builder and live by CASH ONLY**.

How do you determine the value of a dollar? Most people have never considered how important it is to understand economics and the value of money. If you decide to live without this knowledge you can become a victim of your own financial conditions. Economists have been fantastically successful in making people believe that economics is actually a lot more difficult than what it really is. If you are willing to learn, you can gain the skills and confidence you need to be a wealth builder.

No matter the current condition of your finances, this book will assist you in creating a wealthy mindset and lifestyle with a greater sense of ease and well-being. You can dispel any beliefs that may have put you in a place of being a financial victim and create new beliefs that will put you in a place of financial empowerment. The evidence of success is not whether others judge you to be successful. The only evidence is whether or not you did what you intended or attempted to do.

Wealth is a product of labor. Capital is an effect, not a cause; a servant, not a master; a means, not an end. Wealth should never be desired as an end but simply as a means of accomplishing an end. Success is contingent upon a higher ideal than the mere accumulation of riches. Those who aspire to such success must formulate an ideal for which they are willing to strive.

Wealthy people become wealthy and are able to remain that way by using definite principles that can be learned. When you follow a good recipe for making a delicious cake, measuring the ingredients exactly and following the secret recipe to the letter, you will always bake a delicious cake. If you study the principles involved in the process of becoming wealthy and follow them exactly, becoming wealthy can be almost as easy as baking a delicious cake using a recipe. It just takes a little longer to become wealthy because it is a process and a learned habit.

Our desire is for you to achieve the results in living a Built To Prosper lifestyle. This is serious business, so take your time in understanding and applying the principles in this book. It is not good enough to just have hopes and desires to succeed; you must meticulously plan your financial goals and work at them until they become a reality. Too often people see obstacles as roadblocks instead of opportunities.

Unbending belief and faith are the essential elements of bringing your vision of living a financially-free life into physical reality.

Understand that money mastery is the ability to control your thoughts, habits and discipline in regards to your finances. It all begins with responsibility. **Accepting responsibility is one of the hardest of all disciplines, but without it, no success is possible**.

If your finances are not where they need to be, you must recognize that your current circumstances were created by you and YOU can choose to change those circumstances at any moment. All things are possible for you, if you are willing to apply yourself, develop the right mindset and you are committed to achieving your financial goals.

Persistence is self-discipline in action. Now is the time to start living at your financial peak potential. You must go the extra mile and strive to live financially smart. You will have the kind of life you deserve: one that is free from debt and one that you have wisely put into action. The key is to learn and apply the basic wealth principles and watch as your finances increase.

A right mental attitude toward money takes effort, patience and discipline. This Money Mastery attitude must be cultivated. You must feed your mind with positive, nourishing thoughts about money. If you have a negative attitude toward those who are financially free or wealthy, do not expect to join the community of wealth builders. That negative energy will keep you from flourishing. You can't expect to succeed if you are blaming others for getting in the way of your financial well-being.

Many people never attain their financial potential because they have a poor self-image. They don't believe they deserve to be wealthy. People who see themselves as unworthy cannot imagine ever being any better than they already are – which, according to them, isn't much. If you feel like this, you'll have to change your thinking to be able to grow.

There is a direct correlation between what you think, the words you use and the life you have. In order to change your life, change your story. **Reprogram your mind with faith, hope and expectancy that you will join the elite club of those who live a financially free life.**

The principles in this book are not new; you have heard most of these principles before. What is unique about this book is that the information is put together in a way that is understandable and applicable to anyone. **We all must deal with money while we are here on this earth.** If you desire good food, a nice home, reliable automobile, clean water, gas, central air or any amenity that adds comfort to your life, it requires money. M-O-N-E-Y.

This book will present viewpoints which all are related to using wealth building strategies. It does not matter what your current financial status is, it can get better if you "decide" to change your attitude and habits about money and learn to apply the wealth strategies on a consistent basis.

Make this book your daily companion. Develop the right attitude about money by applying the principles we have provided. If you apply them consistently, you will get measurable results. The key is to change your concept of self. As soon as you succeed in transforming self, your world will dissolve and reshape itself in harmony with that which your change affirms. **You are transforming mind into a wealth builder. There can be no outer change until there is first an inner change.**

Let me be totally honest by admitting that I have been flat broke before. I have had those times when I was altogether stressed about how I was going to pay the bills that were very past due! I have likewise had times when I have had more than adequate income to pay all my bills and purchase boats, pay for automobiles with cash and take big vacations. I have had both of the experiences in a matter of months. I'm going to explain, really simply, what I have done to return into alignment with producing more than enough income.

We have used the principles in this book to achieve more than we ever dreamed, imagined or desired. We have found what is truly important in life and we are still in awe of the unlimited possibilities that lie ahead. This is not just for us or a select few; we just applied the principles and got results. Our desire is for you to develop a wealth building consciousness that cannot be taken away.

You Deserve To Be Wealthy

Discover what it means to be truly wealthy. Don't look outside yourself at material possessions, money, and titles. Don't focus on what you lack; instead, look at what you have. One way to find true prosperity is to live as though you already have it. **All that you need is within YOU now, it just need to be cultivated.**

There are two types of people in the financial world, those who are wealth builders, and those with excuses why they are not. Most people read financial self-help books, hoping someday to find the magic formula to make them rich. They believe that if they do what the book recommends they will have what they want and having it automatically makes them into that successful person. Unfortunately, most people probably will not apply the strategies on a consistent basis, because it is not a natural thing for them to do. The 'doing' of it just does not fit with their image of who they are. People will do whatever is necessary to avoid being uncomfortable. Anything great worth achieving will always be outside of your comfort zone. Be comfortable with being uncomfortable.

Learning how to think out of the box is a developed skill that a lot of people think they possess; however, very few really do. Many individuals have been exposed to this type of thinking and comprehend it, but it doesn't mean that they all apply its teachings. Your thoughts are the indicator of the future.

What you think, feel and dream flows inward, then outward. Everything that happens to you in your external world happens because of what is occurring in your internal world. Are you prone to having pity parties for yourself? Do you feel that no one else understands your financial situation? Some people use self-pity as a tactic to avoid taking responsibility.

There is no one to blame. If you are not willing to accept that you created your financial situation, then you really can't get to where you want to be. As long as you are having pity parties about those circumstances they will remain powerful enough to control your life. The moment you accept responsibility, you will have found the power to change it. But as long as you hold on to your victim story, you are powerless.

The first time you stop yourself from having a pity party it will be tough; but do it, and then do it again. Emotionally, you will have burned those pity party bridges. At the end of the day, you have to live with yourself, and if you are not living true to who you are, then in the long run you won't succeed.

Rich in Liabilities and Poor in Assets

The greatest misconception about being wealthy is that you have to flaunt your wealth to show people that you are wealthy. Believe it or not, there might be wealthy families in your community and you would never know it. That is because most wealthy people live like regular people. They own a comfortable home and drive inexpensive automobiles. They prefer to invest their money into assets, not liabilities.

Wealthy people stay rich by living like they're broke and broke people stay broke by living like they're rich. **People who tend to try to flaunt their wealth may be rich in liabilities and poor in assets**. A five-million-dollar home may make its occupants feel wealthy, but if they have no source of income they won't feel well-off for long.

In order to be wealthy, you have to understand the difference between an asset and a liability. An asset is something that helps produce economic value. By owning this asset, it adds value to your overall net worth. A liability is something that you owe money for, it's an obligation. It takes money out of your pocket and decreases your net worth.

If you have the desire to be wealthy, you have to acquire as many assets as possible and do away with as many financial liabilities as possible. Those who recognize this principle have a great advantage in the financial affairs of life. They do not waste time or money on objects that can be of no possible benefit to them.

Wealth builders are concerned with educating their family on the importance of having a good financial education. This is how wealth is passed from generation to generation. They know that their children are not going to study financial skills in school on how to produce profits with their ideas or businesses, or learn the principles they need to build or maintain wealth.

We receive no formal education in the most critical of all life skills - how to become wealthy. **Did you ever, in all your years of public education, attend the class: Wealth building 101? Why isn't such a class mandatory in every school?**

Many people don't learn the financial facts of life from their school or family. They do absorb, from various media and friends, lots of messages, values, and attitudes - many of which they may vehemently disagree with. Consequently, it is your responsibility to teach your family the real rules of wealth. Instruct them in the importance of financial literacy. **We really have two basic choices in life; we can either share knowledge or keep it to ourselves.**

We have come to understand that whatever enters the mind through the senses will impress the mind and result in a mental image which will become a pattern for creative energy. These experiences are largely the result of environment, chance, past thinking and other forms of erroneous beliefs and must be subjected to careful analysis before being entertained. Erroneous statements are made about money and wealth on a daily basis and "poor" thinkers take them and accept them as fact. They do not bother to check the facts for truth; it is much easier not to.

On the other hand, we can form our own mental image of what wealth is through our own interior processes of thought regardless of what other people try to tell us what wealth should be; and by this, we can control our own financial destiny. Once we understand the forces that are acting on us, we no longer have to fall victim to them.

To make a positive change in your financial life, you must empower yourself. The key is to increase your financial awareness. Your power to manifest wealth is directly corresponded to the amount of financial awareness you have. Becoming wealthy depends on shaping the right financial habits and taking the correct steps over and over again. It is no accident. The more knowledge you have about the bad habits you want to overcome, the more successful you will be in conquering them.

The Power to Learn

To learn effectively, you must be internally and externally ready. In other words, the things going on in your mind and the things going on around you must all be conducive to learning. Internally, you need to be motivated and curious. **The state of your internal (mind) becomes a reflection of your external (environment). When you stand before a mirror, YOU are looking into the eyes of your best friend and your worst enemy. Who YOU invest the most time in, will determine the outcome of your life.**

Our problem is not with the seed, but with the soil. Seeds are being sown (wealth ideas) all the time, but the soil (mind) in which it is being sown is not right, so the seed cannot flourish. Prepare the soil (mind) and the seed will produce a harvest. Wealthy people possess wealth consciousness, that is, they have perspectives and habits that help make them rich.

You will not become rich by saying, "I am a millionaire." You become rich by developing a wealth consciousness.

Empowerment is what gets you started. Purpose is what keeps you focused. Commitment is what gets the job done. If you choose today, and it is a choice to become a millionaire, do not expect a million dollars to show up in your mailbox tomorrow. It will not happen like that, any more than you would expect to pick an orange from a tree the day after you planted it.

Not what he wishes and prays for does a man get in life, but what he justly earns. His wishes and prayers are only gratified and answered when they harmonize with his ACTIONS. When your thoughts and actions are clearly and confidently centered on a desired result, all that is good and right will be drawn to you by your own thinking. Do not forget, it is all the same to the world. It is law.

If you have the desire to be wealthy, you must study the acquisition of wealth and apply the principles. Until you move out of your comfort zone and develop the habits that would give you the experience you need to succeed, it is not possible for you to grow and become capable of building wealth. Most people want to become wealthy but instead they continue to practice the habits that would keep them broke. People have emotional relationships – good and bad – with money. **When you get in touch with your negative financial thinking, you can change it**.

You are a living magnet, constantly attracting the things, people and circumstances that are in accord with your thoughts. Your most important "success" is within your own mind. Belief is the key to the basic mind power that turns dreams into realities, the mental into the physical.

God and Wealth

Before we begin, let me make this clear: your relationship with God is personal and is between YOU and God. How you spend time and connect with God is up to you; this is your personal relationship with your creator. We are sharing biblical principles regarding wealth that we've studied and applied to our life.

The key to abundance and financial transformation for the better is a deeply ingrained belief. In the Bible, **Mark 11:24** it states: *"What things so ever ye desire, when ye pray, believe that ye receive them, and ye shall have them."* Notice that there is no limitation, "What things so ever" is definite and implies that the only limitation that is placed upon us in our ability to think, believe and receive.

God wants you to abound and it is His blessings that enable you to accumulate wealth. Here is a key principle in biblical economics: *"You may say to yourself, "My power and the strength of my hands have produced this wealth for me." 18But remember the Lord your God, for it is he who gives you the ability to produce wealth"* **Deuteronomy 8:17-18** God is the author of our abundance. In the Bible, He laid down a firm foundational plan to teach you how to become wealthy. Keep in mind that these are God's words, not mine.

The Bible teaches a practical, everyday way of life. One of the cardinal tenets of the Bible is that you determine, mold, fashion and shape your own destiny through right thought, feeling and belief. It teaches you that you can solve any problem, overcome any situation, and that you are born to succeed, to win and to triumph.

In order to discover the royal road to wealth and receive the strength and security necessary to advance in life, you must cease viewing the Bible in the traditional way. Why has God given us this clear plan for increasing wealth? Surely it is not just so we can buy a nice home or drive a new luxury automobile, although God is not opposed to these things. God's basic desire for us is that we grow beyond simply being blessed to become a blessing to others.

Wealth, joy and happiness are God's gift to mankind that must be stimulated to manifest itself. Because of pride, laziness and being influenced by negative people who limit their expectations, some people will fail to achieve wealth in abundance that God has reserved for them. If you desire to be exceedingly rich it can be achieved with hard work, and obedience to biblical principles that will guide you on the path to unlimited wealth. *"Both riches and honor come from thee, and thou reign over all; and in thy hand is power and might; and in thy hand it is to make great, and to give strength unto all"* **(1 Chronicles 29:12).** God will help those who are willing to make the effort to help themselves.

Your Personal Relationship with Money

In order to bring about wealth, you have to work out your own personal relationship with money. Work out how you feel about money. Learn which beliefs about money are holding you back from financial success. You must understand the human and emotional side of your relationship with money. Consider who you are, what matters to you, your values and beliefs including those about money and how they affect how you handle your finances. No matter what strategy we share with you in regards to building wealth, you can only go as far as YOU think you are worthy. You have absolute control over one thing, and that is your thoughts.

"We don't have to be smarter than the rest. We have to be more disciplined than the rest." -- Warren Buffett

Insecurity and fear are the major mental road blocks that will impede you from achieving financial success. You should not let these elements dominate your thought process that will trigger negative reaction. A determined decision should be made to renew your mind about money and replace those negative thinking with positive, optimistic and constructive thoughts. With this renewed mindset, you will be able to persevere under the most unfavorable conditions and attain your targeted goal. **Wishing and hoping without action will not fulfill that desire.** You must activate your mental and physical capabilities to their fullest potential, to prevail successfully on this financial journey.

Prepared Mentally to Build Wealth

Many financial experts state that being prepared mentally is the recipe for success when building wealth. When one's mind is correctly prepared, the psychological effect of turning into a financial winner is greatly heightened. Readiness comes in many different forms. In order to understand how to be a winner financially, you likewise have to understand how people lose financially. Valuable lessons may be acquired by learning from other people's financial loses as well as your own.

It is significant to remember that losing is not an indictment of your inability; instead, it ought to be viewed as a learning tool utilized to better your financial skills. Most of us learn through episodes of trial and error, consequently transforming failure into a prerequisite for achievement.

It is hard, if not nearly inconceivable, to succeed financially without first developing a distinct set of financial goals. Formulating financial goals is your blueprint for success and one of the first steps to winning financially. Envisioning success is simply as crucial as establishing an honest set of goals. If you cannot see yourself as a financial winner, you will never succeed. Remove the roadblocks that keep you from your desired path by recognizing that you are worthy of wealth. Through awareness, understanding and a desire to change, you can increase your chances for financial success.

Those who have the power to envision themselves as winners are committed to the process and is willing to take action.

You have to think like a financially free person before you can become one. Regardless of what you wish to accomplish, whether it is singing with a rock group, starting your own business or becoming wealthy, abide by these steps and you will soon be well on your way to the life you have always conceived. Financial freedom simply requires that you change your thinking and have money work for you instead of you working for money.

Do You Act or Dream?

Either you are building for expansion or you're hustling your excuses. You can't do both. The main reason most individuals do not accomplish their goals is that they do not know what they want. Self-help author Tony Robbins stated: "One reason so few of us achieve what we truly want is that we never direct our focus; we never concentrate our power. Most people dabble their way through life, never deciding to master anything in particular."

Wealthy people are totally clear about why they want to build wealth. They are unwavering in their desire. They are totally dedicated to creating wealth. As long as it is legal, ethical and moral, they will do whatever it takes to build wealth. I know you may be questioning this statement and I guarantee you it is not based on your own belief, it's probably something you picked up from a broke relative or on TV.

No matter what you think, you must understand that it takes ethics to build wealth. We are not saying that there are no unethical people who have built wealth, but they are not our focus. Wealthy people do not send mixed messages to the universe, poor-thinking people do. What differentiates those who go after their goals from those who don't are a set of daily habits and a unique way of thinking that has helped them build the foundation for the kind of lifestyle they choose to live.

"Your beliefs become your thoughts, your thoughts become your words. Your words become your actions, your actions become your habits. Your habits become your values, your values become your destiny." **Mahatma Gandhi**

If your predominate mental attitude is one of wealth and appreciation you shall find that your environment will reflect the condition that are in correspondence with these thoughts.

If your attitude is of lack and ungratefulness you shall find that your environment will reflect the condition that are in correspondence with these thoughts. **The power is in your thinking!**

Cast out thoughts of failure from your psyche as soon as they come up. There is scientific evidence that favorable thought does work, so turn over that fact if you have temporary doubts about accomplishing your financial goals. Will it be easy to overcome those thoughts of doubt when your bills are due and you barley have enough to cover your expenses? Absolutely not; if it was easy, everyone could and would do it. It takes work to overcome these circumstances.

Planning long-term change is not hard, but making and maintaining the actual change is difficult. You are capable of moving from where you are now financially to a brighter future, the key is to develop a financial plan of action and stick to it. Planning isn't so much about predicting the future as it is about trying to shape it.

Envision the desired result. Keep your goal perpetually on the "front burner" until you achieve it. I can almost guarantee you that 85% of self-made millionaires did not travel through the road to success in hopes of becoming a millionaire. They started slowly and worked their way up to the millionaire's club. As their success grew they built on that momentum. **Their focus was on the wealth building process, not the million dollars. Momentum is a journey, not a destination.**

Learn from other successful people. Talk to people who have accomplished the same goals you are going after. No one succeeds alone. Good relationships can help you grow and improve as a wealth builder. If you wish to be wealthy, contact other wealthy people or join a networking group where they discuss wealth strategies. Other people might be aware of your situation and your needs and may be able to give appropriate advice. By finding out how others achieved the same goal, you will learn what to do and what to keep away from. Wealthy people invest their time and money toward things that would help them grow because they realize that without knowledge, power is nonexistent.

The Power of Ambition

Our culture cannot seem to make up its mind about the value of ambition. On the one hand, we praise those who work hard and accomplish their goals. On the other hand, we put people down and classify them as being selfish and power-hungry, and we frequently take pleasure in seeing powerful leaders fall. No wonder so many people have distorted feelings about being ambitious.

Society tells most people to strive for something other than their personal goal. They start doing what society tells them to do, they become pretty good at it and then one day they wake up and wonder why they are so miserable. Instead of living according to others' expectations, decide to live according to your authentic needs and deepest desires. Being ambitious is not about being selfish, it's about being productive.

Ambitious people understand the value of time. In order to invest a great deal of time into your dreams, you must absolutely love what it is that you do. **Why be miserable chasing someone else's dream?**

Knowing what you need to accomplish to make your life fulfilling and meaningful is not enough. You must act. Discover and follow your path every day. Your power, your instincts, and your ambition will guide you. The challenges, difficulties and obstacles along your path are not negatives to be overcome. They are opportunities for growth and learning.

The lack of ambition is a sign that you are protesting against doing something that you know is right for you. The challenges that you will face are part of the process. Welcome these opportunities to progress further on your wealth building journey.

Everyone has been in a position where they have failed in their financial goals, especially me. But understanding how to approach your financial goals is what makes your goals a long-term endeavor rather than a swift dead end. By being consistent in your daily disciplines and by building upon that consistency, you can achieve new and greater heights.

Think about what you would you do if you could accomplish anything and did not have to worry about money:

_____

_____

_____

_____

_____

_____

_____

_____

Do you have someone who will hold you accountable to your goals? You could ask someone you trust to help keep you accountable. Nevertheless, nothing may take the place of honoring your intentions to yourself. You'll be astonished at how your self-esteem and sense of achievement will increase when you accomplish your goals. The problem most people have when pursuing a financial goal is that they look at the number of steps in front of them to reach their goal, rather than observing the overall picture. They see the faults and mistakes they make along each step they take, while failing to realize that those failures have slowly been building the foundation for the level of success they soon will have.

"You hold the keys to every door; the vision for your future. And it is when you realize that this power exists, your life will be in good hands: God's and your own." **The CEO Roundtable**

Are You Afraid to Fail?

Don't let your fear keep you from going after your goals. Fears are opportunities for learning. When you face them and move forward, you develop courage, strength and confidence. Be forewarned: as you progress, you will face new fears. Look at the possibilities, and move past the fear. Transform your fears. Ask questions about them.

The key is to never give up on your financial goals and to keep pressing forward. Realize there will be moments when nothing will ever seem to go your way, moments when all you see are unpaid bills. But if you keep pushing forward, if you refuse to stop, there will be sunshine after the storm has passed. Fear of failure may be a dream killer. Becoming cognizant of your fear is the first step in addressing it.

People can become wealth builders with the help of a mentor, or they can learn through the process of trying and failing, until they get it right. Most people dislike the idea of failure, but, if you really think about it, the only way not to fail is by not trying.

"You cannot put a time limit on success, it is a process. It takes time to create an idea that will move the world. The process is long and hard and it is not for the weak. You are going to "cry" many nights but know when your time has come, the joy will compensate for it." **The CEO Roundtable**

Don't Try To Fit In... Be YOU!

Trying to get everyone to like you, will set you off on the road to mediocrity. Once you perpetually attempt to be the person other people want you to be, you cheat yourself out of individuality and your own aspirations. Dance to the beat of your own drummer. Don't just blindly follow everyone else.

If you cannot control outside conditions, you are able to control your response to them. If you are currently working in a dead-end job with a boss who is demanding and does not value the contribution you bring to the organization, make a conscious effort to tell yourself that their poor management skills may make you upset only if you let it. Working for the wrong people can drain the life right out of you.

If your place of employment is not going to help you reach your financial goals, you may want to consider becoming an entrepreneur. In order to have what it takes to be an entrepreneur, you must be willing to lose everything you have to gain everything you desire. **A majority of wealthy people have built their wealth through entrepreneurship.** If you're not willing to learn what it takes to be wealthy, no one can help you. If you're determined to learn, no one can stop YOU!

Successful people never limit their learning to only when they are told; they learn because they know that when you choose not to grow, you are working against your true nature. **Become a student for life and you will never stop growing.** When you were young, your curiosity led you to explore and learn. We want you to recapture that curiosity now by studying the strategies for building wealth.

Network with Wealth Builders

You are who you network and associate with. If your acquaintances all live paycheck to paycheck, then your power to have a wealthy mentality will be limited to a paycheck-to-paycheck mentality. The key is to network and build relationships with people who can help you grow and challenge you. I'm not telling you to disassociate with your current friends. *Bring them a long for the journey if they want to be wealth builders as well.*

Successful people network with like-minded individuals whose goals are also aligned with theirs. They seek out the people who will elevate them to the next level to bring out the very best in them. Unsuccessful people will network and connect with those who bring no value to the relationship. Choose your friends wisely, because you are *"the average of the five people with whom you spend the most time with."*

Avoid negative people. Do not allow anyone the opportunity to douse their negative energy on you as you try to evolve financially.

Allowing other people to have power over your thoughts, feelings and behavior drains your mental strength. **You hand over your God given power when you allow what other people think about you, to control how you think about yourself.** Giving away your power has a negative impact. You have to protect your mind at all cost.

Your environment and the people with whom you come in contact tremendously influence your attitude. If you want a consistent, positive attitude, surround yourself with things that inspire and empower you. If either your environment or your associations are negative, change them. Spend time with other positive, successful people in places that are conducive to success; this makes it easier to cultivate a wealth builders attitude.

If someone makes you feel like they are pushing you beyond your own limitations that is when you are in the presence of greatness. I know this from experience; my mentor does this to me every day. I have always had great mentors in my life who gave me the support I needed when I got a little side-tracked.

Give yourself permission to be wealthy. You don't know what you can accomplish until you try. So try!

The mission is to take care of yourself and those you love. You can't take care of others unless you first take care of yourself, and manage your own responsibilities. Once you master your issues and carry your own load, you're ready to help others.

"All of life and its achievements, its possibilities, depend upon our consciousness, and we can develop any sort of consciousness." **Orison Swett Marden**

Read this book carefully, earnestly and diligently. Each chapter will show you how to use the wealth building strategies that the financial elite use. We have taught these strategies to men and women all over the world. Prove to yourself the amazing way these strategies can help you. It could be, and we believe it will be, the turning point of your financial life.

ASSET
MONEY
FINANCIAL
PROFIT
CHART
SALE
EXCHANGE
MARKETS
SUCCESS
ECONOMY
ACCOUNT
REPORT
CRISIS
BUSINESS
MANAGEMENT
FINANCE
RESEARCH
INVESTMENT
INVESTOR
ACCOUNTING
MONITORING
COLOR
WEALTH
SHARE
BALANCE
HAND
PENSION
LIST
PLAN
INDEX
COMPANY
FEMALE
MARKETING
WOMAN
ANNUAL
CONCEPTUAL
GRAPH
GRAPHS
HUMAN
BANK
FUND
PRICE
CASH
GRAPHIC
TRADE
IDEAS
PEN
SAVING
BONDS
PROPERTY
FIGURES
DEPOSIT
CURRENCY
REPORT
TAX
TREE
ECOSYSTEM
GRASS
SAVE
SOLAR
GROWTH
ENVIRONMENT
ENVIRONMENTALLY
ENVIRONMENTAL
ECONOMICS
INFORMATION
DATA
PAPERWORK
CALCULATION
COMMERCE
BANKING
EARNINGS
DIAGRAM
ECOFRIENDLY
CALCULATOR
CONCEPT
NUMBERS
VECTOR
STATISTICAL
ANALYZING
LIFE
FUNDS

CHAPTER I:
DEVOLOPING THE WEALTH BUILDERS MINDSET

Your attitude matters! To work to improve yourself, you must deeply believe that you are worth the effort. You can do very few things effectively if you feel negative about yourself. Most people with a low self-esteem or feel unworthy of wealth don't try to grow.

We have to build up the inner YOU before we can get to the money! Self-esteem is the value you place on yourself. You affect your self-worth with judgments about yourself that are usually much more critical than other people's judgments would be. The goal, of course, is to feel worthy, valuing yourself for who you are and loving yourself unconditionally regardless of your financial status. Everyone is worthy of being valued as a person.

What happens to you financially, will not define you as a person. What will define you is your attitude about your experiences. **YOU are more valuable than the money. Without YOU the money has no meaning**.

I know what it is like to go from living in abundance to barely getting by. I was born in the beautiful city of Brooklyn, New York! My father was a business owner, who owned a grocery store and apartment buildings and my mother worked as an office manager. Our financial circumstances changed when my parents split and my mother decided to move to South Carolina to be close to my grandmother. This was a culture shock for my brother and two sisters. We were not prepared for the lifestyle change.

We went from living a very comfortable lifestyle to living in the projects. My mother held several jobs to try to get by but it wasn't cutting it. My siblings and I wasn't use to my mother saying "we can't afford it." **It was like she was speaking a foreign language**. We were accustomed to having nice clothes and having an abundance of food in our home. This all changed in the south!

It got so bad that we had to get on public assistance. I remember the first time my mother tried to send me to the store with food stamps. I told her I wasn't going and it earned me a nice beating. I could never get use to not having access to money. I would call my father back in New York to ask for money. But those calls became less frequent, because my father made me realize that I could not keep using him like he's a bank. It took me awhile to understand that he was teaching me a lesson. **In life, if you want something, you have to go out and earn it.**

I am grateful for my experience in the South. It made me resourceful and this is where I learned my sale skills. I sold pecans, cucumbers, watermelons and I mowed lawns. By the age 13 I was earning $500 a week selling candy in school. I was known as the candy man. My ambition wouldn't allow me or my family to settle for less. Knowing the right thing to do provides no advantage unless you actually do it.

It does not matter what kinds of things you have done in the past. The only thing that matters is what you are doing now. The only thing that will define you as a person is how you are living your life NOW. There are no barriers, no walls in life that can't be crossed.

Each of us is in control of our own journey – deciding where we want to go and how to get there. You are the only one who can use your ability. **It's YOUR responsibility**.

Your Beliefs About Money

The way you see life will largely determine what you get out of it. How you were raised and what you heard growing up has shaped your attitude and beliefs about money.

Many people believe these negative sayings:

• Money is evil

• You have to sell your soul to be rich

• Money can't make you happy

• You can't make a ton of money honestly

• Rich people are greedy

Actually, the truth about money is that everyone needs it, creating wealth is perfectly fine and being rich can be a wonderful thing. It's just that most people are too lazy to learn what it means to be wealthy. Your pursuit of wealth will require you to purge the negative beliefs you have about money and its connotations. **You really can change your beliefs!** You are the one who developed them and gave them their importance as rules for living, and you can change them.

You succeed – or fail – according to the quality and content of your thinking. Your greatest asset or liability is your mind and how you use it. **No mind ever receives the truth until it is prepared to receive it.**

In order to reprogram your mind to accept higher levels of wealth, you must discover what beliefs have limited your experience in the past, and you must consciously decide to change those beliefs.

You get the best out of life, when you give the best of yourself. **You are the product of your own thoughts. What you believe yourself to be, you are**.

It is not your intelligence, your education or your circumstances that have left you financially unsatisfied, but your limiting beliefs about what it means to have financial freedom. It's important to figure out how money functions in your life. Nothing creates a greater gap between successful and unsuccessful people than the choices we make. If you are serious about being wealthy, you will have to learn how the wealthy think.

Review the below questions and answer them as honestly as you can:

- What negative associations do you have regarding wealth?

- Do you feel that wealthy people are stingy or greedy?

- Do you feel that wealth will cause conflict in your life?

- Will money ruin some of your friendships?

- Do you believe you can handle the responsibility of wealth?

Whatever it is, you must find out what has held you back from financial independence, and you must consciously decide to change those beliefs. **What beliefs have held you back?** Try to get at your core belief about money. For example, an erroneous belief for many people is that "money is the root of all evil." The correct Biblical quote is from **1 Timothy 6:10** which states; *"For the love of money is the root of all evil."*

Many people believe that poverty and prosperity both come from birth or luck. And this is false. Both poverty and prosperity are a mindset. You can have $10,000,000 and still feel poor and you can have $5 in your account and feel prosperous. As we stated earlier, it's all about attitude.

The best news of all regarding financial success is that nature is neutral. We all play an important part in determining our own financial success. If you follow the rules of money and develop the habits as wealthy people do, you will get the results that wealthy people get. And if you don't, you won't. It is as simple as that.

You cannot allow someone who have no real knowledge about wealth, tell you erroneous myths about money. They will have you believing money is evil and that money will corrupt you. They may even have you believe, it is godly to be poor. **Never let a poor man tell you how to get rich**. *For the record "being poor" is a state of mind.*

You must realize that money is not good or evil; it is a tool for expressing your creative energy in the physical world. Realize that you are worthy of wealth and you will use money for the good of many. Whatever you truly believe will become your reality. Believe you will succeed, and you ultimately will; believe you will fail and you surely will.

If you believe wealth is your birthright, then you are more than likely to create wealth. If you believe that money is scarce and hard to get, then that reality will manifest in your life. When you accept limiting beliefs about money, they gain control over your life. Positive beliefs about money can produce positive results: negative beliefs will produce limiting and unwanted results. There is a specific cause for every effect and everything happens for a reason, even if you don't know the reason or cause.

Our self-talk about money is based on our beliefs.
A mind that is not properly prepared for finances is a terrible thing to waste. The best possible investment you can make in your future is to invest in your financial education. No one is going to sit you down and go over the A, B and C's of money. You are considered fortunate if you grew up in a household where your parents had positive open conversations about money. But for those who did not, your investment in your financial education is of the upmost importance.

It is time for you to take personal responsibility for your financial future, because neither the government nor your job will take care of the things that matter most to you. The basic things we all want are a stable financial future, a stable family life and good health. It is natural to want the best for you and your family, the best foods for your body which is your temple, the best clothing and the most comfortable home filled with all the amenities you desire.

"Many people completely fail in life or are forced to live in mortifying poverty, to struggle along perhaps under the curse of debt, miserable and handicapped all their lives because they never learned finance for themselves." **Orison Swett Marden**

What is Money?

Money is commonly defined as a medium of exchange. Someone once said to me, "Money is not everything." My reply was, "Go tell your mortgage and credit-card company that." Money brings power to the user. **Money has no power in itself but having control over how it will be used gives YOU power.** Money is used to build beautiful cities, powerful armies, help oppressed nations, feed the hungry and build a thriving economy. *"Money isn't the most important thing in life, but it's reasonably close to oxygen on the 'gotta have it' scale."* **Zig Ziglar**

There is nothing more important than for someone to be able to earn their living; however, knowing how to use money to your best advantage is equally vital. While some people would have no problem splurging their money on frivolous things, wealth builders would think twice and hold off on spending. That is because we all relate differently to money, depending on the level of influence we've had from our upbringing, friends, and the living standards of our society. You could call this your "money mindset."

The more money we have, the more power we have. Money is meant to be used with a strong sense of discernment and wisdom. In order to handle large amounts of money, you must be mentally prepared to handle it. **The use of money and the things it can buy will control you if you do not have the right mindset for it.**

Studies show that no more than three people out of a hundred who have made money know what to do with it and are able to hold on to it. If you need further proof, study the people who have won the lottery. Most of the winners end up worse off than before they gained their winnings. Why? They were not mentally prepared for the riches they received. They gained a large amount of money but they had the wrong money mindset (easy come, easy go). They never developed the proper philosophy of saving and investing their money; they had the hand-to-mouth mentality.

Who is in Control of Your Money Mindset?

However, you make your living, whether your income be small or large, you will always be placed at a disadvantage unless you have the proper mindset in managing money. No one can choose the time when financial opportunities will come their way. But you must be emotionally prepared to seize such moments when they occur. Being emotionally prepared means sensibly understanding the fortunate circumstances, evaluating the risk and confidently taking action to benefit from the event.

Too many people let financial opportunities pass them by because their fear paralyzes them and they cannot get beyond their financial comfort zone. **No one can be successful or happy, no matter how optimistic, if they are forever living under the stress and strain of overwhelming debt.**

Many people are motivated by money. It is not wrong to be money motivated as long as you are not controlled by money. Accumulating wealth in order to help others and earning money for the advantages it can offer you and your family are worthwhile objectives. Having enough money can liberate you from a stressful job, free you to follow your dreams and allow you to take care of your loved ones.

When all of your expenses are covered and you are relieved of the worry that comes with paying your debts, you can devote all your time and energy to the things that really matter to you in life. **Money gives you options in life.**

There is a peace of mind that comes with financial stability. It allows you to set your own agenda for your life. Financial stability eliminates many of the "what ifs" associated with money worries. The more money you have, the more choices you have. By having choices, you will no longer feel overwhelmed, boxed in, and unable to do anything about a situation. Are you ready to give yourself more choices? Don't limit yourself. Having choices keeps you in control.

Getting ahead requires the right attitude: the "Wealth Builder's Mindset." It also calls for careful planning. If you want to change the effect, you have to change the cause; your thoughts are the ultimate cause. With the right mindset and financial habits, you can overcome any financial obstacle.

Everyone has experienced a financial setback; how you handle it makes all the difference. When life deals you an unfavorable financial hand, don't sulk or complain. Assess the situation and act quickly to make things better. Don't let obstacles interfere with you getting ahead financially. Never quit when the going gets tough. Instead, use bad events as learning experiences. **Never stop growing because life will never stop teaching.** Each challenge you overcome makes you stronger.

Your Internal Dialogue about Wealth

What stories do you tell yourself about your wealth? That you must work extra hard to earn it? That you have no time to create a financial plan? That being wealthy is an impossible dream? If this is your internal dialogue, then you should not be surprised if it is also your external reality. You probably did not realize how often you speak to yourself about money and how it affects your financial experiences. If you tell yourself that you are a financial loser (your story) and your mind will accept it. Then it will do everything possible to help you fulfill your negative story.

If your story is one of constant triumph over tough odds, you will almost surely overcome any and all financial obstacles. It is what YOU tell yourself that will determine your future. Many people give away their power by following the advice of someone who've never built or created anything. When it came to building wealth, I only listened to my mentors who've demonstrated the wealth principles in their life.

Here are some ways you can begin using positive self-talk about money to develop a wealth builder's mindset. The first step towards creating positive money self-talk is to become more aware of how you speak to yourself about money on a daily basis.

The following strategies can help you become more conscious of your personal money self-talk blueprint.

1. Carry a note pad with you throughout the day and jot down your thoughts about money when you think of them.

2. Write a bulleted account of your thoughts on money throughout the day and a general description as to the experience that led to the thought and the experience that came after the thought on money.

3. At the end of the day, go back and reflect on the words that were chosen while speaking to yourself about money and how you can add positive language to describe money which will lead to more positive experiences in regards to the use of money.

Your new wealth building internal dialogue will become real the more you focus on it. Success in wealth building requires intense commitment, engagement and focus. It means total dedication to the present, not to some vague future. When you hear yourself saying something negative about money, just say "delete" or "I rebuke that" Just as if you typed an error on your computer and you hit delete to erase the error, do the same with a negative statement that may come out of your mouth. We were taught this strategy by a very successful entrepreneur from Montana and it has worked for us ever since.

As you notice yourself saying something positive in your mind about money, you can continue your thought and be able to reflect on it positively by smiling and saying to yourself, "I Am the Master of Money." Saying this aloud with feeling will be more powerful, and having to say it aloud will make you aware of how many times you are infusing positive self-talk thoughts. The truth about money is that if you have enough of it, you hardly think about it; but if you lack it, you will think of nothing else.

Never say that you can't do something, or that something seems impossible. We are limited only by what we allow ourselves to be limited by: our own minds.

We are the masters of our own reality; when we become self-aware to this: absolutely anything in the world is possible. As with any new habit, you need to work hard to embed your new wealth building internal dialogue into your consciousness. Self-affirmations like: "I am a wealth builder" or "I attract only lucrative, enjoyable and beneficial opportunities" are particularly empowering because they increase your sense of peace about money in any given situation, and they give you the ability to search for solutions. Open your consciousness about wealth which will make you more hopeful and will release your imagination to new possibilities.

Confidence Building for Becoming Wealthy

"I always knew I was going to be rich. I don't think I ever doubted it for a minute." – *Warren Buffet*

Being confident in oneself is one of the key criteria to become a wealth builder. Look at the confidence aura exuded by Warren Buffet when he expresses the statement above. It is not a coincidence that he built Berkshire Hathaway into the business it is today. If you believe you cannot become wealthy, you will speak and act consistently with that belief; and in most cases, "prove" yourself right. Similarly, if you change your expectations of the world to reflect your infinite potential for wealth, you will quickly generate the thoughts, feelings and actions that will draw money to you. If you want to become wealthy and stay wealthy, you need to begin thinking of yourself as someone who deserves great wealth.

You must begin by feeling rich within, in order for it to manifest outwardly. As you begin to truly see yourself as wealthy, you will begin to develop financial habits that will help you grow. To attract more money, you need to remove all negative associations about money. Today's question is: How do you build up your confidence level to propel you to achieve your financial goals?

The key is to set smaller and achievable goals for yourself at the beginning of your path to wealth building. No, we are not thinking small. In fact, you should think BIG! **The point of doing this, is so that you can develop the proper habits that lead to financial success.**

Your confidence grows as you achieve your smaller goals, once accomplished then you set bigger financial goals for yourself. As you continuously hit higher and higher goals, your confidence will also skyrocket! When I first started on my journey to building wealth, my first goal was to open a savings account. I know this may seem simple to you but I didn't have a savings account. I thought the best way to save money was to put it in a shoe box. The day I went to open the savings account, I was nervous.

The bank teller asked me "How much to you want to deposit into the account?" I said "How much are you charging me to open the savings account?" She looked at me kind of weird and said "It's FREE and you'll earn interest in your money." I said "I guess I'll deposit all of it" and handed the bank teller my shoe box filled with $5,500.00. I was excited! I accomplished my goal of opening a savings account. My confidence grew as I deposited more money into my account and as my money grew I looked for more ways to earn more interest. When you understand the financial game, you will love when your money works for you to earn you more money.

Wealth building is a journey not a marathon. Imagine if you just started a new business venture, and you set your target profit at $1,000,000 in the first six months. What would happen if you did not earn a single dollar in the first six months? You would probably quit, and your confidence would hit rock bottom. Many people give up on their journey to financial freedom because they expect things to happen overnight. They expect the money to be rolling in right away. I have never met a wealth builder who became wealthy overnight.

They developed the habits and put the work in. There are some people who may have gotten rich quick, but I guarantee you they spent that money just as quickly. Pardon me, if you thought this book was going be filled with a whole bunch of fluff. We want you to win, our goal is to share with you the strategies to win, not fill you up with false hope. I have read many books that fill you up with all kinds of weird stuff and none of it worked. That is why when it comes to sharing strategies, I only share what has worked in my life. The quickest way to wealth is to learn from those who are wealthy.

Financial Success Box and Success Journal

On your journey to financial freedom, we would like for you to record all your financial successes. You can do this by creating a success box and investing a success journal. Within your success box include the debts you've paid off, any accomplishments, testimonials and thank you letters from clients (everything positive!) into the success box.

Within your Success Journal record all your successes daily, regardless of how small or how big they are. Every day ask yourself and write your response in your success journal: **"What did I learn about money today?"** Go through the items in the box or the journal when you need motivation, as we tend to forget how far we have come at difficult moments. Your financial success box and your success journal will be your guide when you get a little side-tracked on your journey. We all get in a little funk at times, but when you have things in place to lift you up, when you are down, you won't stay there for long. Use your financial success box and your success journal as an empowerment tool.

Learn from Financial Winners

Associate with like-minded people who are also working on building wealth. It is essential to put yourself in an environment conducive to grow your confidence and to keep you motivated. There is no better place to be, than among a group of people who are also trying to achieve the same goals as you – financial freedom. Join new social and networking events to expand your network! Not only will you be able to exchange ideas, you will also be able to find people who can hold you accountable to your goals.

How to Poise Yourself to Become Wealthy

Step 1: Commit – Are YOU committed to being wealthy?
YOU must accept that you want to be wealthy, and you do not need to make any apologies for it. Wealth builders are different from the people who procrastinate on their financial goals. Wealth builders are committed and have higher determination in accomplishing their financial goals. You cannot leave your financial stability in the hands of someone else. The power is in your hands, it's your responsibility. By accepting the change, you need to be committed, and be willing to take persistent, consistent, and massive action.

Step 2: Save – Do YOU have a savings plan?

Develop the habit of saving money. It does not matter how much as long as you make it a habit to save a portion of your income on a consistent basis. Without savings, you will never have money for any form of investment opportunities. Besides, you can never be wealthy, if you spend everything you've earned. Start saving early. Nest eggs are a lot easier to build if you start when you are young. **The key is to start NOW!** Pay yourself first with automatic deposits to saving and investment accounts.

Step 3: Adopt the Wealth Builder's Mindset

Wear a wealth builder's hat and THINK wealthy. A wealth builder never blames other people or the economy for what happens to them, even when they suffer a financial loss. Instead, they work to improve themselves and learn from their setback. Those who have developed a wealth builder's mindset see opportunities and hope when others see failures.

Step 4: Follow Your Passion – Are YOU doing what you love?

Do what you are passionate about and you will never work a single day in your life. There is joy, when you are following your purpose. Most people spend their entire life working a job they are not passionate about.

In contrast, most successful individuals have something in common. They enjoy what they do. You will not find a wealth builder who detests what they do. The solution to reaching your wealth building goals is to own what you invest in. The success that comes with doing what you love, far exceeds that earned by someone who eschews risk by working for other people. Wealth builder's control their destinies and focus on what they want in life. Taking ownership means controlling and allocating your resources through thoughtful, deliberate action. **Remember, do not chase after money; do what you love and money will chase after YOU!**

Step 5: Create a Clear Financial Plan

How much exactly do you want to earn monthly? Yearly? How will you pay off all your debt? How much do you need to achieve financial freedom? Setting your financial goals is imperative to ensure you have a clear destination. Without a financial game plan, you will not be able to visualize your dream of financial freedom as attainable. It's not sufficient to just say, "I want to be rich" because it does not give you a clear picture of a financial goal. Do you want to own assets that are valued over a million dollars or do want to be worth a million dollars? These are two different things. You can own assets valued over a million dollars but you can be five million dollars in debt.

Step 6: Learn How to Manage Your Income and Expenses

Do YOU know how to manage a budget? To be a wealth builder, you need to know how to balance both your income and expenses. Track your income to make sure it is utilized on the right and necessary things. One mistake many people make is that when their income increases, they also increase their expenses. Most people's financial woes derive from spending more than they make, not from having insufficient income. If your outflow is greater than your income, no matter how much you earn, you will remain broke.

When you are a wealth builder, when your income increases, your savings and investment opportunities increase. Keep Track of Your Spending – examine your bank and credit card statements for the previous months and analyze your spending habits. Uncover where your money is going and if it is going towards unnecessary purchases, learn to develop the habit that will lead to financial success. Financial planning and money management is not complex. The key is to save and spend less than you earn. It is a habit, not rocket science.

Finally, take MASSIVE Action!

Take massive action to supercharge your financial plan – make it a reality! Plans can look good on paper but if you don't act on them, then they are useless. Start with small consistent steps, and aim higher after each successive step. Not only do wealthy people act fast, but they also think before they act. If the opportunity to take action presents itself, they will take it and never allow any regrets to invade their thinking. Never wait at the door of opportunity, open the door and go in.

You are able to dramatically increase the overall quality of your life far faster than you might think possible. All you need is the desire to change, the decision to take action, the discipline to put into practice all that you have learned and the decision to persist until you get the results you want. Among the most important personal choices you are to make is to accept 100% responsibility for everything you are and everything you will ever be. This is the first-class turning point in wealth building.

Accepting complete responsibility for your life means that you refuse to make excuses or blame others for anything in your life that you're not pleased about. You refuse, from this moment onward, to criticize others for any reason. You refuse to complain about your financial situation or about what happened in the past. You eliminate all your if-only's and what-ifs and center instead on what you truly want and where you are going. This decision to accept complete responsibility for your financial results, with no excuses, is absolutely essential if you desire to enter the Wealth Builder's Club. From now on, regardless of what happens with your finances, say to yourself, **"I am responsible."**

Secrets of Wealth Building Millionaires

Millionaires are normal people just like YOU! They breathe the same air, and have the same twenty-four hours as you do. Wealth builders who are "millionaires" do things differently. They use unconventional approaches to reach their goals, regardless of their circumstances, and they assemble teams of partners and mentors to make their dreams a reality. Wealth building millionaires have different habits, qualities, and ways of thinking than the average person. These habits are most prevalent when it comes wealth building.

Wealth building millionaires set their sights on what they want to achieve. Set clear goals for yourself. Imagine yourself being a millionaire and what you would do to achieve it. As Robert Collier says, "If you see yourself as prosperous, you will be. If you see yourself as continually hard up, that is exactly what you will be." Everything has to start somewhere, so make your first step and move ahead! **Yes, YOU can be a millionaire! If you aren't a millionaire yet, you should be.**

Wealth building millionaires work on their passion. According to research conducted by Thomas J. Stanley, author of *The Millionaire Mind*, more than 80% of the millionaires surveyed admitted that they would not have been successful if their vocation was something they did not care about. Look at the wealthy people who seem to be always succeeding - Warren Buffet, Oprah Winfrey, Bill Gates, and Earvin Magic Johnson. They all talk about their work passionately. The question now is: What is YOUR passion?

Wealth building millionaires educate themselves. One major hurdle to earning money is to not fully understand how money works. Do you know how to read your bank statements? How much do you know about money management and investing? If you have zero knowledge on investments and money management, how do you expect to become wealthy? You do not need to be a qualified financial adviser but you do need to have some basic knowledge about how money works. So, spend a little time each week reading the money section in a financial publication such as Forbes or Money magazine. Read one financial book a month on investments. If we spent as much time researching financial matters as we do researching the next flat-screen TV or which new mobile phone to buy, we would all be a whole lot richer. As Jim Rohn correctly pointed out, "formal education will make you a living; self-education will make you a fortune."

Wealth building millionaires grow their money. Life is a constant struggle if you live from pay check to pay check. The way to build wealth -- is to make your money work for you. Where millionaires invest is as important as how. Instead of spending money on things that aren't practical, wealth building millionaires put their money towards essential items that will continue to increase their wealth.

You put money away today because you expect to have a tomorrow, and putting your money to work is better than having your money sit in an account that is not earning you any interest. Wealth building millionaires work smart to earn extra money from investing where their money will in turn "work hard" for them. For example, they grow their money by investing in businesses, stocks, bonds or real estate. **Key Principle:** *Only invest in what YOU know and understand.*

Wealth building millionaires are willing to take risks. If you read the biographies of self-made millionaires, you will realize many of them have often gone through countless failures. What makes them who they are today is their persistence and their never-give-up attitude! They try and try and try and then, one success pushes them up to the top! Wealth builders have a unique way of thinking that actually helps them earn even more money by making wise financial decisions. Sooner or later, the man or woman who persists succeeds.

As you look back over your life, do you wish you would have trusted in yourself more, been a little courageous and been less cautious in the chances you took?

Use Affirmations to Develop a Millionaire Mindset

An effective way to develop a millionaire mindset is by using affirmations – declarations that resonate with you. Wealth is simply a subconscious conviction on the part of the individual. You will not become a millionaire by saying, "I am a millionaire, I am a millionaire." You will grow into a wealth consciousness by building into your mentality the idea of wealth and abundance. To him that hath the feeling of wealth, more wealth shall be added; to him that hath the feeling of lack, more lack shall be added. Your subconscious multiplies and magnifies whatever you deposit in it.

I built up several affirmations for myself, taking the qualities I most needed and affirming for myself over and over again: "I am healthy, wealthy and wise." I kept up this affirmation, always the same, never varying, until I could wake up in the night and find myself repeating, "I am healthy, wealthy and wise." It was the last thing on my lips at night and the first thing in the morning. Not only did I affirm it for myself but also for my family and for others I knew that needed it. I want to emphasize this point: whatever you desire for yourself, affirm it for others as well.

Every morning as you awaken and right before you go to sleep at night, deposit thoughts of wealth, abundance, prosperity and peace. Dwell upon these concepts. Busy your mind with them as often as possible. Be bold enough to claim that it is your right to be wealthy and your deeper mind will honor your claim. These constructive thoughts will find their way as deposits in your subconscious mind and bring forth abundance and prosperity.

Here are 6 affirmations to develop a wealth building millionaire mindset:

1. I am a superb wealth magnet.
"For as he thinketh in his heart, so is he." **Proverbs 23:7** To become a wealth building millionaire, you want to draw as much money-making opportunities to you as possible.

2. I manage all my income with ease.
"For which of you, desiring to build a tower, does not first sit down and count the cost, whether he has enough to complete it?" **Luke 14:28, ESV** To be wealthy, you need to know how to be an excellent money manager. It is pointless to earn millions if you end up spending it all.

3. I take consistent action to increase my wealth.
"What doth it profit, my brethren, though a man say he hath faith, and have not works? can faith save him?" **James 2:14** One must be committed and be willing to take action to achieve their goal of becoming a wealth building millionaire.

4. Wealth flows to me endlessly.
"Surely goodness and mercy shall follow me all the days of my life: and I will dwell in the house of the Lord forever." **Psalm 23:6** One of the most desirable situations to be in, for anyone, is to have a steady flow of goodness flowing their way.

5. My ability to earn money increases exponentially day by day.
"Enlarge the place of thy tent, and let them stretch forth the curtains of thine habitations: spare not, lengthen thy cords, and strengthen thy stakes." **Isaiah 54:2** You want to be able to accumulate your knowledge on wealth creation on a daily basis so that you can implement them to earn your millions!

6. I become wealthy by adding value to other people

"Give, and it shall be given unto you; good measure, pressed down, and shaken together, and running over, shall men give into your bosom. For with the same measure that ye mete withal it shall be measured to you again." **Luke 6:38**
One must not only become wealthy but also teach other people how to become wealthy as well. When you look at people who are at the top of their field, you will discover that they all have one thing in common. Can you guess what that is? They all create value for others and in doing so; they also create success for themselves. This doesn't happen by accident; it is 100% intentional.

What Would YOU Do?

I want you to think about something very seriously for a moment: If you could design and create your personal financial lifestyle, right now, how would it look? Would it be having all of your debts paid off? What type of home would you live in? Would you continue to work a job? Where would you go to spend quality time with your family? Really take the time to visualize these things. *Thoughts become things. If you see it in your mind, you will hold it in your hands.*

We have all had moments in our life when we procrastinated on being productive for comfort and peace. This is when we chose to seek an average comfy lifestyle rather than to explore the possibilities of our potential. This is the art of procrastination, and it is a vicious cycle that never ends until you are willing to make the decision to abandon it.

Nothing comes closer to mediocrity than a man or woman who chooses to wake up on days filled with endless opportunities and possibilities only to throw it away on procrastination. And the worst part is that it is hard to leave a lifestyle where you expect nothing more for yourself. Breaking the procrastination habit is not easy. After all, if it was simple, we would have more people becoming entrepreneurs and wealth builders instead of people settling in life. The urge to put things off can be strong, especially when there are so many things around us that are a distraction to our productivity.

People will always talk about how they are going to change their financial circumstances but when push comes to shove, they will not take the necessary action to get it done. It is not that they do not have the motivation or drive to pursue it; it is because they are so accustomed to procrastinating that to change in their daily routine is like trying to win the lottery. People can talk all day, but it is through action that you will get results. If you are going to succeed financially, begin to take action in any form; because the sooner you leave the state of procrastination, the less it will haunt you in the future when you are forced to act without a choice. It is hard to go from mediocre to great, but much easier to go from good to great. Make the leap easier for yourself, one action at a time.

Does Wealth Make You Happy?

If you follow your desires and ask yourself why you truly want the things that you want, you will find that your desires always lead to the attainment of certain emotional states. For example, right now, you may desire to be wealthy. But what is it that wealth will give you? Do you really want the millions of dollars saved as a physical symbol of your wealth? Or do you actually desire the feelings you think you will have if you possessed enough money? The answer is obvious. You do not want actual money; that is, bits of colored paper. What you want is freedom, independence, the ability to share, to solve problems and to provide for yourself and others. Ultimately, you want to be secure and happy. These are feelings, not things.

These are emotional states that you desire. And why do you desire these states? Because you want to give more, have more and experience more. So, you should look upon your desires as positive, growth-inducing emotions. Are wealthier people happier, or are happier people more likely to be grateful and content? If happiness, freedom, security, and independence is what most of us desperately want, it should be a major goal for society.

Unfortunately, we are often conditioned to feel guilty for wanting too much. Many believe that there is a blatant contradiction between wanting to have it all and feeling empathetic to the plight of less fortunate people. Basically, we are led to believe that it is evil to be rich in a world filled with poverty. This attitude misses a crucial truth of humanity. Evolution is an individual experience, and each individual must learn for himself or herself how to manifest more of the life energy we all desire. We cannot help others by being pulled down by the "reality" of the world's suffering.

Empathy does not mean you must be as poor as someone else to be able to help them. The truth be told, you cannot help anyone being poor. True empathy means that you use your God-given power, your hopeful energy and your wealth to solve the situations of the world that you find unsatisfactory. Only when each individual stake their claim to divine power can negative physical experiences be alleviated.

There is one emotion that is the cause of the lack of wealth in the lives of many, and most people learn this the hard way: It is envy. For example, if someone you know is doing well financially, does it make you envious? Do you compare your lifestyle to theirs? When you compare your life and finances with those of others, it can lead to deep personal unhappiness. Instead of making parallels between your life and others', judge your success according to your ability to earn a living, pursue mastery and discover purpose.

If it upsets you when someone else is succeeding, don't expect to succeed. YOU can't have what you despise. To entertain envious thoughts is devastating because it places you in a negative position; therefore, wealth flows from you instead of to you. Comparing yourself to others creates a totally unrealistic measure for what constitutes wealth. If you are ever annoyed or irritated by the success or wealth of another, claim immediately that you truly wish for him/her greater wealth in every possible way. This will neutralize the negative thoughts in your mind and cause an ever-greater measure of wealth to flow to you by the law of your own subconscious mind. You don't really want anyone else's life. You just want your own life to be better. You can improve your life right now by no longer comparing yourself with others.

The 10 Causes of Financial Failure

1. Lack of Financial Education. Financial knowledge includes understanding how a checking, savings, and investment accounts works, knowing the difference between earned and passive income, what using a credit card really means, and how to avoid debt. The understanding of finances impacts the daily decisions an average family makes when trying to balance a budget, buy a home, fund their children's education and ensure an income at retirement.

Many people do not take the time to invest in their financial education. Research studies across countries on financial literacy have shown that most people (including entrepreneurs) do not understand the concept of compound interest, and some consumers do not actively seek out financial information before making financial decisions. 40% of working class adults would grade themselves a C or below for their knowledge of personal finance.

Most consumers lack the ability to manage a credit card efficiently, and their lack of financial education is responsible for their lack of money management skills and financial planning. Your level of financial literacy affects your quality of life significantly. It affects your ability to provide for yourself and your family, as well as your contribution to your community. Financial literacy enables people to understand what is needed to achieve a lifestyle that is financially balanced, secure, sustainable, ethical and responsible. Stay true to your values, yet always be open to learn. Your financial success is in YOUR HANDS!

2. A Negative Attitude Toward Money. One may believe that having plenty of money is wrong due to the misinterpretation of the scripture: *"For the love of money is the root of all evil."* **1 Timothy 6:10** It is difficult to earn money if there is a negative attitude about it or if you have erroneous beliefs about wealth. You cannot attract something that deep in your heart you despise. This is a most common attitude for many people. They desire money but their attitude is negative, they do everything within their power to sabotage their financial success.

If you want to earn a large amount of money, you first have to get rid of all negative thoughts and attitude about wealth. With a negative attitude toward money, you will believe it is bad to have it and might even make some errors of judgment that would cause you to lose money. On the other hand, if your attitude is positive and you are open and willing to have wealth in your life, you will attract money through various income producing opportunities.

3. Lack of Self-Discipline with Money. The most difficult thing for most people is controlling their spending. If you cannot control your spending, then no matter how much money you make, it will never be enough.

The lack of discipline in finances usually leads to debt, which is the #1 cause of stress. Without discipline, you will never be able to build wealth or join the financial elite. Discipline is being able to say no to impulse purchases. It is being able to do the things you do not want to do when you know you must. It is forcing yourself to do the things that are necessary to secure your financial future. The only way to keep from going backwards is to keep going forward. Discipline is the price of success. There are three steps and each one is absolutely essential: You must first have the knowledge of your power; second, the courage to dare; and third, the faith to do.

4. Trying to Keep up with The Joneses. Many people live beyond their means because they cannot bear to have other people think that they cannot afford certain luxury items. It used to be that spending money on status symbols for the sake of flaunting your wealth was an activity reserved for those who had the money to flaunt. That has all changed, since people now have access to credit. They've upgraded their life with debt. For many, "keeping up with the Joneses" became an overwhelming obsession that led to financial ruin.

Overspending is usually a psychological problem that manifests itself as a debt problem. People buy things that they think they should have because culture says that they are important (a certain make and model automobile, designer clothes, etc.). **Key strategy:** Before you make a purchase, ask yourself: "Am I really using this money in a way that is going to be a benefit to my financial future?" Is this an asset or liability? Be willing to make sacrifices when it benefits the bigger goal: financial freedom.

5. Lack of Vision for Financial Future. A person with no clear goal on what they want to accomplish financially is headed towards financial disaster. You cannot expect to have a vision for your relationships, your health, your spiritual life, and yet neglect your finances. Money is important, no matter what others may say or what you may believe. To operate in this world, you are going to need money so why not have a plan for it? Your goals are not the same as anyone else's and they do not have to be. The key is identifying what you want, setting priorities and making a plan. When you get clarity in your vision, it gives you energy. When people get a grip on what they are going to accomplish and where they are headed, it sweeps away many mental roadblocks to action.

6. Comfortable with Being an Underearner. Do you earn less than your potential despite your need or desire to do otherwise? If so, you may be an underearner and all the budgeting in the world may not help you until you address the underlying issues that are holding you back. Those who are comfortable with being an underearner lack the ambition to move past mediocrity. Many people complain about not earning enough income on their jobs, but they are not willing to do what it takes to earn more. Why accept a job that is not paying you what you are worth? You cannot blame the job; you are the one who accepted the position. If you want to earn more, be more and do more, so you can have more. Are YOU willing to invest in yourself, to develop the skills needed to be a wealth builder?

7. Selfish with Money. A person who has no desire to share with those less fortunate will not achieve high levels of prosperity. They see giving money to those in need as a loss and less as a duty. The more we give, the more we shall get; we must become a channel whereby wealth can flow through. I am not saying to go out and just give your money away. You must use wisdom when giving money; there will be many people who will try to take advantage of your kindness and then there are those who just want to keep their hand in your pocket.

Those who are selfish only look out for themselves. You will find that broke people are more selfish with money than wealthy people. Broke people see giving money to charity as a financial loss or they make the excuse that they have nothing to give. Wealthy people see giving as an obligation; they look for ways to spread their wealth where it can be of greatest service to mankind.

8. Forget Who Is the True Source of Wealth. *"If you start thinking to yourselves, "I did all this. And all by myself. I'm rich. It's all mine!"—well, think again. Remember that God, your God, gave you the strength to produce all this wealth so as to confirm the covenant that he promised to your ancestors—as it is today."* Deuteronomy 8:18, MSG

What does the phrase "power to produce wealth" mean to you? Many people put money before their health, family and spiritual beliefs. God is not bankrupt and we who are the representatives of God's power should not be bankrupt either. Our relationship to money is then a reflection of our relationship to God. The source of my wealth is God. It is sometimes easy to forget that God is the source of all things, including our money and possessions. When I go to the bank, cash a check or receive any form of value as an increase in my wealth, I look to God as my source. Look within to the true source of your wealth. Be grateful for things in your life that represent abundance, health, wealth, happiness, and all the blessings that are already present.

9. Fails to Take Responsibility for Financial Circumstances.
Have you ever met someone who blames any and everybody for their financial problems? I know someone like that, and he has a great deal of money. I am struck, every time we meet, by his failure to take responsibility for what is happening in his financial life. Everything is someone else's fault. Every problem is explained away with reasons about why he cannot affect the situation or the outcome. If we deny our mistakes or fail to take responsibility for our finances, we fail to learn and improve. People who take complete responsibility for their finances experience joy and control of their money. They are able to make choices because they understand that they are responsible for their choices. The most important aspect of taking responsibility for

your money is to acknowledge that managing your finances is your responsibility. No one can be financially smart for you; people have their own issues with money they need to work out and they cannot take on your responsibility. You are in charge. Many have lost touch and disregarded the basic financial principles – to spend less than you earn and invest wisely for great returns. No matter how hard you try to blame others for the financial events of your life, each event is the result of the choices you made and are making.

10. Borrows Money with No Plans or Means to Pay it Back.

Borrowing money and not paying it back can and will ruin your reputation. When someone has to call a person a hundred times to get the money back that they lent, it can put a strain on the relationship. I have lent money to friends and family members and borrowed money from friends and family members, and neither situation worked out well. I learned a lot from both experiences.

Most importantly, I learned that I will never loan money to friends or family members again; I would rather have them work for it. I have loaned money to a family member and when they did not pay me back, family get-togethers became very awkward. *"Be not thou one of them that strike hands, or of them that are sureties for debts."* **Proverbs 22:26**

Many people are being squeezed by the stress of their debt and lack of financial discipline. They cannot get a good night's sleep without thinking about their debt. The bill collector is always calling and harassing them for the money that they have borrowed. Debt is not worth the stress; it is not worth the headache. Just as it pays to invest your money wisely, it also pays to make your debt payments wisely.

Debt Steals Money from YOU

If you are in debt, you are wasting massive amounts of money — money you ought to be utilizing to produce wealth for you and your family. So, paying off all your debt is absolutely a worthy goal. "Debt is bondage."- **Cashology Academy**

Getting out of debt essentially means getting out of bondage. However, as frustrated as you are with your current financial situation, many often find it difficult to act effectively against debt. By being discipline and budgeting are the most important thing you can do to help you achieve your financial goals. There are people who earn plenty of money but are broke, because they do not manage their money well. The key is to be disciplined in your money habits. You must create a plan and stick to it.

List all of your financial obligations. Begin by making a list of all the financial obligations you have, and make sure you include the family member you borrowed money from and then determine in which order you will pay them. You can start by paying off the debt with the highest interest rate or the lowest the balance. This is your decision and responsibility. The feeling you would get after paying off that first debt will be exhilarating.

If you are going to be a wealth builder know the difference between wants and needs. We all have those moments that after we have accumulated a little savings that we want to purchase a new car, new home or we just want to ball out. But, is this necessary? Or, do you just want that splurged to show your friends that you got it? Sure, it would feel good for a moment. But, it doesn't benefit you financially in the long run. Instead of spending money on things that aren't practical, wealth builders put that money towards essential items that will continue to increase their wealth. If your destination is to join the financial elite club, it is going to require discipline.

What will your life be like when all your bills are paid and you have more than enough money in your account? How would your life be different? Attempt to really feel the freedom you will have. Do this each time you view your goals, particularly when you first wake up and prior to going to bed. **You must do the work.** Wealth will not come to you out of the sky, neither will it drop in your lap. Envisioning your goal is great, but there is work that will need to be done.

Get your family involved. Unless you live alone, your goals will more than likely affect those you live with. So, if your goal is to become wealthy, you will most likely require the cooperation of your loved ones. After all, it does not do much good if you are attempting to build wealth and secure your financial future and your spouse is in the mall splurging every weekend. Make it a point that your goals are shared and the individuals who may affect the result endorse them.

Joining the club of the financial elite is a process. Many would have you believe that you can get rich overnight but it does not work that way. There are many bad habits and erroneous beliefs you will need to overcome. This is why you must keep your goals in front of you, envision it as much as possible, and track your outcomes frequently.

KNOW THY CASHFLOW

My Income	My Expense
Earned Income $	Rent/Mortgage $
Business Income $	Property Taxes/Insurance $
Interest $	Internet $
Dividends $	Cable $
Residual Income $	Car Payments $
Bonus $	Car Insurance $
Commissions $	Other Loan Payments $
Real Estate Rentals $	Health Insurance $
IRA $	Day care/Elder Care $
Life Insurance $	Gas/Oil $
Other $	Water $
	Telephone/Cell Phone$
	Grocery $
	Transportation/Gas $
	Car Maintenance $
	Education $
	Personal Expenses $
	Other $
Total Income $	**Total Expenses $**

Action 1: Minimize your expenses. Categorize ALL your expenses into either: (a) fixed expenses, e.g. home, car note; (b) necessary-but-not-fixed expenses, e.g. gas, phone bills; (c) variable expenses, e.g. clothes, gadgets, dining out. Cut down or remove as many expenses as possible from Category (c). Save as much as possible from Category (b) e.g. by investing in a fuel-efficient car, commuting by public transportation or choosing a mobile service package that caters to your need.

Action 2: Develop a wealth building budget and most importantly, stick to it. Contrary to common notion, it can be pretty simple to start a wealth building budget and maintain it. We have created a wealth building budget spreadsheet for you. All you need is 10 minutes a day to update your wealth building budget spreadsheet, and the investment of 10 minutes daily is well worth it. They key is to increase your income and assets and decrease your expenses and liabilities.

Action 3: Pay off your debt. Start paying back either with the smallest debt or the biggest debt. Small debt is the fastest to be paid off; nevertheless, the satisfaction can be overwhelming if you manage to pay off your largest debt first! Consider creating a savings and investment account so you can build to pay off your debt. Name this account "The Debt Payoff Account."

Action 4: Increase your income. Find out if you can increase your salary from your current employer, e.g. by working overtime. Alternatively, explore other ways to generate income, e.g. starting a small business or joining a network marketing business. Establish a part-time business – increase your earning by doing something on the side and enjoy what it is that you do, as this can be an avenue that you will earn additional revenue which can be used for investment purposes. Many people start small businesses and expand gradually as they take the time out to understand what they are doing. Many self-proclaimed millionaires gained their wealth through this medium. Do keep your expenses at the minimum even as your income grows.

Action 5: Don't accumulate any more debt! It is imperative to be conscious that you should not add any more debt to your household at this juncture. You are wealth building, not debt building.

Action 6: Change your spending habits, change your life! If you buy a mega-sized Frappuccino daily at your local coffee shop, try making your own coffee at home, which tastes just as good if not better! If you really want to know how much you are spending on coffee, do the numbers. If a cup of coffee cost you $2.50 and you buy it 5 times a week that's $12.50 you are spending a week ($50 a month, $600 a year). You can invest in a nice coffee machine for $75 and invest the difference. The amount of money you save from here could be channelled to clear your debt.

Action 7: Get off the side-line and get in the financial game. Don't procrastinate. Procrastination is the worst habit to develop. The longer you wait the more debt you accumulate and the worse your financial situation will become. In contrast, the sooner you settle your debt, the sooner you can move on to start your journey to becoming a wealth builder.

Our experience with finances comes from our money habits. The key is to know your own "strengths and weaknesses" when it comes to the use of money. The cost of irresponsible use of debt has resulted in people accumulating low credit scores, foreclosures on their homes, damaged marriages and sometimes, even the loss of one's sanity.

The good news is that it does not have to be that way. It all starts with a decision, a decision to become a wealth builder instead of a debt accumulator. A wealth builder's mindset can literally transform the lives of all who live by its power. Your financial stability is totally dependent upon your ability to make wise decisions and take action.

Don't let ego or stubbornness get in the way of you becoming a wealth builder and achieving financial freedom. When you open your mind and you are willing to learn, you'll enter into the land of opportunity and wealth!

SAVINGS
SAVE
INVESTMENT
FINANCE
CURRENCY
ECONOMY
CONCEPT
BANKING
CASH
HAND
MONEY
FINANCIAL
PIGGY
BUSINESS
BANK
PINK
NATURE
GROWTH
WEALTH
DISCOUNT
COIN
DESIGN
COMMERCE
THETIME
BEAUTIFUL
PERSON
HAPPINESS
WEDDING
SHAPE
VINTAGE
ARROW
CLOCK
TAG
PENNY
DECORATION
GRAPHIC
PEOPLE
HOUR
FLOWER
MINUTE
RICH
CRISIS
LOVE
INVESTING
SYMBOL
PIGGYBANK
LABEL
BANNER
GOLDEN
HAPPY
PROFIT
SALE
SECURITY
RIBBON
CLASSIC
PROFESSIONAL
HOLDING
SUCCESS
EARNINGS
INVITATION

"The real source of wealth and capital in this new era is not material things... it is the human mind, the human spirit, the human imagination, and our faith in the future." - **Steve Forbes**

CHAPTER II
THE PRINCIPLES OF BECOMING A WEALTH BUILDER

Cultivating habits that lead to financial success and putting your money to work on a regular basis is not only important, it is also something beneficial to the overall lifestyle and mindset of a wealth builder. Habits are created by repeating enough steps enough times to train the habitual mind. The mind learns through repetition and reward rather than from listening to explanations. That is why we focus on taking consistent action in this book. We are helping you develop the habits of a wealth builder. The discipline factor alone is well worth practicing as it will help you develop stronger skills for future commitments.

Ideally, a working adult should be able to comfortably save about 20% of his or her income. If this habit is successfully developed, then the individual would be able to venture into other types of investment opportunities. If the habit of saving is not developed, then becoming a wealth builder is a mere dream. Wealth building can be learned. It is a muscle and once you learn to flex it, there's no end to what you can accomplish financially. Attempting something and accomplishing it aren't the same. When you are determined to be a wealth builder, nothing can stop you. It is empowering to realize you have more control than you ever knew over what you achieve in life.

When something is a priority in your life, you have to be willing to walk away from anything that's standing in its way. Keeping within a planned budget will allow you to comfortably create a savings plan that will be useful in times of need. These needs can be when a job is lost, when medical emergencies arise, when a good deal comes along, when opportunity strikes and any other positive venture that might require instant access to considerable funds. Thus, learning to develop the habit of saving will eventually prove to be beneficial both in the present and for future opportunities. Drawing up a savings plan that can be put into practice over a yearly time frame would eventually help you create a healthy savings account. Take one small step every day to initiate a lifelong positive habit. You form habits over time through repeated behaviors.

Saving money is an important part of a healthy financial future. Life is not predictable and knowing that you have cash on hand for unexpected needs, a down payment for a home or for investment opportunities, can be both comforting and vital during economic shifts. Additionally, you can play an important part in teaching your children about saving by helping them open their own savings accounts. Creating and sticking to your savings plan can help you meet your financial goals. With the right knowledge and strategy for change, what previously seemed as an impossible financial goal becomes rather straightforward and possible.

Reasons to Save More

Start saving early. Wealth is a lot easier to build if you start when you are young or NOW. Learning to save as much as possible is always a good habit to form; thus, there is no real need to have a reason to practice this positive wealth building habit other than for its sheer benefits which are rather extensive. However, if you need a reason to save more, the following are just some of the more prominent ones to go by:

- Having a healthy savings account is always beneficial. This will help you tap into this resource when the need arises, compared to having to resort to taking out a loan which will only incur high interest rates that may cause the wealth building process to be severely affected. Setting aside money for unexpected life situations ensures that you can pay for emergencies without going into debt. A healthy savings account can bring you peace of mind when things get challenging. What would you do if you experienced a job loss or personal financial setback? The goal is to save enough to cover your living expenses for at least six months to a year.

- Creating a good long-term savings plan will also allow you the option of making a huge down payment, if you decide to purchase a home; thus, eliminating the need for larger loan packages and higher interest rates. When you have the money, you are able to bargain better. Cash is King when it comes getting a better deal. **Banks love to give money to people who don't need it.** Building equity through home ownership is an essential part of accumulating wealth.

- Saving more will also allow you to have the resources to invest in income producing opportunities when they are available. People often miss opportunities simply because they lack the resources to capitalize on them. Therefore, learning to save more and frequently putting aside any excess cash will keep you from missing out on investment opportunities.

- Making the effort to save more will give you the opportunity to be disciplined and focused, which are traits that will help develop the necessary skills needed to be a wealth builder. The sooner these traits are cultivated, the sooner they will bear positive results. No matter how determined or sincere you are, making life changes is hard. You may intend to be a wealth builder, but intention without action is pointless.

Types of Saving Accounts

Account Type	Description
Regular Savings	You deposit money at your discretion.
Savings Club	You deposit a fixed amount weekly, bi-weekly or monthly.
Certificates of Deposit (CDs)	You deposit a fixed amount that gains a determined amount of interest for a set period of time.
Money Market Account	You deposit a large amount, you receive interest and you may write a few checks each month.

Financial Workout Tips to Get Your Finances in Shape

Keeping track of your personal finances is something that can be practiced or learned with some strategies and careful and diligent observations. There couldn't be a better time to take control of your financial future. **You can benefit from the below strategies when it comes to keeping your finances on track:**

- Being an informed buyer is a good skill to cultivate, as this will be pivotal in ensuring that you do not spend your money impulsively or be taken advantage of by savvy salesmen making impressive sales pitches. The key is to know the true value of any goods and services intended to be purchased before actually parting with your money. There is no shame in doing research before making a purchase. With the use of the internet, you can now price compare and save money. All it takes is a little patience. At the end of the day we have to understand what we are doing with our money and be responsible for making better choices. I manage my financial life like a Corporation and every dollar is an employee. Before an employee (money) leaves my company, I ask myself "is this employee (money) being used in the most productive way that will benefit the Corporation?" The main purpose for all of my employees (money) is to be productive to make the company financially stronger. Whenever you make a frivolous purchase, that's like an employee leaving your company without giving a two weeks' notice.

- Buying on credit is a habit that should either be broken or controlled to its maximum, as this form of making purchases does not allow you to be completely conscious of how much is truly being spent. Let's say you use your credit card consistently without paying off the full balance. You have a revolving balance of $15,000 on your credit card, and your daily interest rate is 0.06% (which is approximately equivalent to an APR of 22%). Multiply $15,000 by 0.06% and you will get $9. You will be paying $9 in interest on the first day. This process occurs each day until the end of the monthly statement cycle. So, at the end of the month, the beginning balance $15,000 becomes $15,270 when the interest charges are applied at 22% APR. The extra $270 in interest could be put into a savings account or invested. That's 270 employees (money) leaving your company on a four weeks' notice.

You can avoid credit card interest by paying your balance in full every month before the end of the grace period (typically between 21 and 27 days). If you fail to pay the entire statement balance, or do not make the payment in time, you would have forfeited the grace period and interest charges will typically appear on the next statement.

YOU should have no interest, in paying interest, only receiving interest on your money. The less money you spend on paying interest, the further your employees (money) will go.

To avoid accumulating new debt, pay credit card bills before or during the grace period, don't miss payments and be sure you understand how your card issuer assesses interest. Don't be shy about asking your card issuer for a better deal. The credit card business is very competitive, and your account is valuable. **Remember: banks love to give money to people who don't need it.**

Understanding interest rates is critical to managing your personal finances in areas like deposit accounts, mortgages, investments and credit cards. In a simple term, the interest rate is a percentage rate the financial institution is going to charge you to borrow money. When you borrow money, the amount you pay back is dictated by the interest rate, plus any additional fees. The same goes for saving, on which you earn interest. Before borrowing or opening a credit account, you should always figure out how much it will cost you and whether you can afford it. Understanding how interest rates work will help you prepare for any interest rates change. Interest rate is a very important financial vocabulary term that everyone should know and understand.

Make Wealth Building Real

If we are aware that the future is uncertain, how should we deal with this uncertainty? Strategy is the art and science of informed action to achieve a specific vision, or an overarching objective for your finances. Creating financial goals is easy but being committed to process of wealth building is something else which requires much more than just some words and thoughts, it requires strategy. As stated earlier, think of your household as one big corporation. The success of your organization depends on the financial health and upward mobility of the people who are a part of this company. Developing sound financial habits increases your odds of building a secure and profitable organization.

Debt will Cost YOU

Debt that you are unable to pay back comes with a cost; your health which is affected by stress. And this is a very expensive price to pay for debt. Before you borrow or use a credit account, determine the cost of this transaction and whether you can afford the payments. If you are persuaded to submit an application for a credit card and you are presently finding it hard to pay your bills, then you need to stop and think about the decision that you are making. **Are you willing to give up your health for debt?**

When it comes to making purchases using cash, you are less impulsive. You only use what you have. If you want to be financially-smart, you have to be firm when it comes to living a wealth builder's lifestyle. Becoming debt free is a worthwhile goal. Some households actually maintain a debt free lifestyle. With a credit card, you have the power to buy whatever you desire at the spur of the moment and it is probably something you do not even need or perhaps, even want. **You can save yourself a lot of heartache, by avoiding the following financial mistakes:** having unrealistic expectations, being impatient and allowing your financial decisions to be influenced by other people who do not have money.

Many of us can relate to making financial mistakes. In life, we can become consumed with trying to keep up with the Joneses. We acquire so much "stuff" we think will make us happy but in the end, it leads to emptiness because we are not grounded on sound financial principles.

When I took responsibility for the financial decisions I've made in life, I took back control. I could no longer blame the government, my job, or my parents. I knew I could either take responsibility or play the financial victim game. I realized that if I take the position of victim, I lose power. If I chose responsibility, then I would have the power to do something about the financial circumstances in my life. The more responsibility I accepted, the more power I attained.

Manage Your Money Well

Many years ago, when I was in the financial industry, I use to train financial advisors on how to build model portfolios to manage their clients' assets. The minimum assets under management needed for the financial advisor to be a part of our program was $25 million. I took a lot of time studying how these financial advisors allocated their clients' assets. I also wanted to know "why" these clients invested in certain companies, created an estate plan, had a family trust and a team of advisors. I learned it was all about strategically building wealth.

Management was the key. From that day, I chose to become a multi-millionaire, and I expected it to happen. I wanted someone to manage my family wealth, but I also wanted to become an informed investor so I could become a strategic wealth builder. Financial experts agree that know-how is the best way to counteract the fear of investing, which often involves the fear of losing money or making a money-losing decision. People tend to fear what they don't know.

You have to think about your future. You need to start thinking about living financially-smart. A financial plan can help reach your destination if you implement its strategies. A financial plan is one of the best tools you can use to live financially smart. The planning process can help you understand your investment goals and your strategy for achieving them. It leads you to face your financial fears and take action steps for reaching your financial goals. The key is to put an end to the accumulation of liabilities and develop the habit of asset building.

Many argue that since they work hard, they deserve to get whatever they want. But if you have to go into debt for those desires, then you are living outside of your means and you are purchasing those desires based on your future earnings which can lead to financial stress. When you make purchases using credit, the interest you are paying on that purchase is taking more money out of your pocket. People who successfully play the wealth building game always look for ways to get good returns on their money, not pay interest on non-appreciating assets.

At first, you may find it quite painful to not be free to buy whatever you want but over time, if you are smart with your money through saving and investing, then you will eventually be able to pay for what you want with cash. It's a wonderful feeling to buy something with cash and not have to worry about a bill later. I purchased my first investment property for $75,000 cash. It was a very large purchase for me at the time, but I knew that my money was being invested in an asset that would eventually increase in value. These 75,000 employees were going to be very productive for the organization. Every dollar you currently have in your account is an employee for you. Find ways to make them be productive.

The goal is to achieve financial freedom, free from debt and worry. It is not suggested that instead of owning credit cards, you load up your wallet with a bundle of cash. Of course, you can use debit cards and secured credit cards if you are certain that you have the money to cover the expenses. I remember when I was working in the financial industry and I received a call from a screaming customer. I answered the phone in the standard robotic greeting, you receive when you call any customer service line. I didn't have time to ask the gentleman

"How can I help you?" before he shouted "What's going on with my account?"

I responded "Can you please provide your account number?" He gave me all his details and verified his identity. When I looked at his account all I saw was RED. In the financial world, RED means trouble. I said "sir, I see your account is overdrawn due to insufficient funds. You have written several checks that have bounced." He responded "How can my account be insufficient funds, when I have more checks?" I had to ask him to clarify, he said "as long as I have checks, I should have sufficient funds." I had to pause for a minute, because clearly this gentleman did not understand how checks work. I explained "sir, if you write a check to someone, you need money in your account to cover." He said "but I have checks." I said "sir, having checks do not mean you have MONEY."

This story is humorous and scary at the same time. After I hung up the phone, I thought someone was pulling a prank on me, but this gentleman called right back and spoke to a financial representative that sat right next to me. I guess he didn't believe me when I told him "having checks do not mean you have money."

The Keys to Managing Your Money Flow Wisely

Whether you are operating a household or a business, it is essential that you are aware of the correct ways to manage your cash flow. As long as your spending equals or exceeds your income, you will never be wealthy. The only way to become wealthy is to continually increase the gap between the amount of money that comes in and the amount that goes out. This is important given that the last thing you want to experience is financial problems. Most people think financial security comes from making more money, but most people spend any extra income they earn.

It is impossible to make an analysis if you are not aware of your exact income and expenses. You must be aware of the balance that you have in order to be familiar with how much funds you have to save and invest. Even when you are operating a business, you could commit big mistakes if you are unaware of the cash flow coming into the business.

You Should Not Run Out of Money

This is a bit of a common sense; however, it is most likely the most basic recommendation that can be given and it is something that a number of people have the tendency to overlook. Rather simply, you have to do all that is possible to steer clear of putting yourself and your family in a financial bind, in view of the fact that if that takes place, you will possibly resort to things you do not want to do. Your initial instinct may be to dip into your retirement fund or access a huge amount of debt and this would only get you deeper into money woes, particularly if you do not have a practical means of repaying it.

Make Use of a Personal Finance Management Program

While you don't have to become an accountant to understand financial statements, you do need to pay attention to your money. It would be great to hire the services of a professional accountant. But you should also have your own personal finances management system as well. The majority of the accounting functions that are needed to manage your income and expenses can be achieved by utilizing a personal finance management program. This is great tools that would make it easy to manage your finances. You can research many of the programs on the internet. You do not need to be a financial expert to use these programs. Many of them have a tutorial to walk you through the process of getting set up.

Living a wealth building lifestyle means you manage your money well and make wise purchases with your money. One of the big mistakes people make when they start to take responsibility and control of their finances is that they fail to assess their personal philosophical values about money. After all, your values ultimately determine how you will earn your income, how you will invest and how you circulate your money.

Money issues are serious and they affect all areas of your life. It is important to have a plan of action for your finances. Learn to be smart with your money and avoid spending on purchases that do not have resale value. You are training yourself to not be naïve enough to spend a future paycheck before you have earned it. It takes discipline to get use to a wealth building way of living. Wealth management is something you really have to devote time to in order to succeed.

Either you give in and conform to the standards of a debt-based lifestyle or stand your ground and stay away from unnecessary debt. In life, you will either be disciplined in your finances or have financial regrets. Being disciplined in your finances is a mental habit and you must choose the mental habits that empower you and serve you. When you focus on living a wealth building lifestyle, you will experience life more abundantly because you will owe no one. We live in a world that provides the most opportunity to be prosperous, achieve financial success, and live a life of fulfillment.

"Every human being has been "Born Rich" it's just that most people are temporarily a little short on money!" **Bob Proctor**

Every decision you make with your money is an investment. To have control over your money and to become the Master of Money, you must develop a wealthy mindset. Wealth is a matter of expectation. **Our thoughts, feelings and attitude about money will always influence the outcome of our finances.** If we expect to do well in our finances, then we will begin to think and act accordingly. Those who amass wealth create a habitual attitude and expectation of wealth.

We get in this life whatever we concentrate on. Our financial success or financial failure is in our own hands. Many who are complaining that the door to financial success is locked by some mysterious rich person, or they have no one to help them to get the position they desire, are not succeeding financially because they are not willing to make the necessary effort to succeed. They make excuses on why they can't "get it done."

They are not willing to do the work required; they want someone else to do the work for them to make things happen. Through our experiences in life, we have seen people who dreamed big dreams but failed to live out those dreams due to their halfhearted commitment to the process of developing themselves and the people they surrounded themselves with. My mentor said: "**He could tell me my financial future just by looking at the five people with whom I spent the most time with.**" I told him my financial future is bright, since he's one of the five people.

To create wealth, you have to learn how to have self-control, have a financial plan and invest wisely. If you study the money habits of the wealthy, you will see a pattern. They only "use" other people's money to acquire assets such as real estate or businesses. This asset will pay back the money which was used initially and they will continue to earn income from that investment. In Robert Kiyosaki's bestselling book *Rich Dad Poor Dad,* he stated: "Concentrate your efforts on only buying income-generating assets." **Key principle: Whatever you do with borrowed money, you should make more income and interest for you than what you have to pay to the lender.**

When you shift your mindset from a consumer to a wealth builder, you change to a new game with a new set of rules. When your game and rules about money change, your whole financial world starts changing. **There are no limits to you attaining your most desired financial goals as long as you can define what it is you want to achieve**.

A great deal of what you have perceived as limits in your financial life are actually limits you have placed on yourself. The good news about this is that you have already begun to eliminate those limiting beliefs. You began the moment you picked up this book. Do not follow the path of those who blame everyone else for their financial woes and make excuses rather than take personal responsibility for their finances. There are people who live according to the wealth building principles, but there is an increasing number of people who lack basic financial life skills and it is ruining their lives.

Wealth building begins not in a bank account, but in your mind. Wealth building is not only a mindset, it is a lifestyle. It begins with your thoughts. Throughout this book, we will continue to give you strategies to work on your thinking. You may see the same statement several times throughout this book and it is for a purpose. Seeds are being planted, once they grow it will change your thinking. *"No great improvements in the lot of mankind are possible until a great change takes place in the fundamental constitution of their modes of thought."* **John Stuart Mil**

There are two ways to change or transform. One is through an emotional impact that jolts us into change and the other is through constant spaced repetition. Think of how you learned to ride a bike. You learned through constant repetition and repetition is the key to success. To be successful at anything in life, you must develop the right attitude. You may face some obstacles or setbacks but it is through your persistence and consistent action that you will achieve your financial goals.

Applying The Wealth Principles of The Money Masters

The approach to wealth creation is different for many people. For a number of them, real estate investments offer a steady inflow of tax advantages and cash flow. To others, investing in the stock market is used as a strategy to increase their nest eggs.

Wealth comes to the man and woman who sees and uses his or her potential for wealth. Chances are that these men and women made a decision to set priorities, to pay themselves first and to build their economic power for the benefit of themselves and their family. In spite of what you believe wealth represents and what approaches you use in wealth creation, according to money masters, there are actually four principles of wealth creation:

- Increase income sources

- Earn more and spend less

- Start early

- Manage risks

What Is Your Source of Income?

When it is time to decide how you can earn more money, it can be difficult to weigh the options: do you spend more time at work earning overtime pay in trying to get a promotion and a higher salary, or do you invest time on a part-time business or passion where you can hustle in your free time and maybe earn some extra cash? Regardless of your personal circumstance, earning extra money is a key component to your financial success. Below are various sources and types of income to lay the foundation for this discussion.

Sources of Income

- **Primary Income (or Earned Income)** - The most common form of income is the money you earn by working a job. In return for your time and effort, your employer provides you with money in the form of a wage or a salary and/or a possible bonus. *You are working for money.* You must trade your time (a limited resource) for money. Once you stop working, the income stops coming in.

- **Passive Income (or Residual Income)** – This is income earned from sources other than your job. This can be money you earn from a side business such as network marketing, online business, real estate investment property or special projects. This is the opposite of earned income. Once you stop spending time on these income sources, the income flows do not necessarily stop. It is called passive income because you don't have to work traditional nine-to-five hours to earn money. This kind of income is the key to wealth building and financial freedom. YOU can earn money while you sleep.

- **Portfolio Income (or Investment Income)** - The money you make from interest, capital gains and dividends - "The money your money makes for YOU."

To begin the process of building wealth, now is the time to think about how you can maximize your income-earning capabilities. Can you create a product that people will buy over and over again? Can you engage others to sell your product? How can you leverage your time to earn income off the efforts of others? The sooner you can answer these questions, the sooner you will have the potential to achieve financial freedom. Diversified income streams build wealth. Some of the wealthiest entrepreneurs have more than 10 income sources. You have to think like a wealthy person before you can become one.

Understanding Financial Statements

When you learn to decipher well-prepared financial reports, you will be much better equipped to understand the realities of your financial position, what you have been doing correctly and where you are facing challenges. To determine your financial position, use financial statements that clearly outline your monetary flows and net worth. The three (income, balance, cashflow) statements offer different perspectives that will give you a comprehensive picture of your financial performance.

Income statement - The income statement shows revenue, expenses, and net earnings. Your income statement tells you if you are making a profit—that is, whether your household or business has positive or negative net income. For this reason, the income statement is also called a profit-and-loss statement. The statement includes three kinds of income: earned income, passive income and portfolio income. When you understand the income and expense components of the income statement, you can appreciate what makes you profitable.

Balance sheet - Shows your liabilities, assets and net worth. While the income statement shows your progress over a period of time, the balance sheet is a snapshot of the moment. It tells you how efficiently you are using your assets and managing your liabilities.

Statement of cash flows - Shows your actual cash position, independent of your income and balance sheet positions. A cash flow statement gives you a peek into the organization's checking account. Like a bank statement, it tells how much cash was on hand at the beginning of the period, and how much was on hand at the end of the period. It then describes how the organization spent its cash. As with a checkbook, spending of cash is recorded in negative figures, and the receipt of cash is recorded in positive figures.

Earn More and Spend Less

Launch your plans now. Dedicate at least two hours a day to a new venture or a business idea that will create a steady stream of passive or extra income. The key is to earn more and spend less. Establish concrete financial and personal goals for your family and your career. Unless you control your spending through the use of a budget, you will not be able to create wealth. I have worked with several people who have worked hard to build a healthy passive income, yet they failed to develop the habit of spending less than they earn. Too frequently, people who generate a million dollars per year wind up with several million dollars in debt. As I stated earlier "Banks love to give money to people who don't need it." Yet some people don't know how to control themselves when they have "access" to credit. Wealth builders hold down spending even as their earnings continue to grow.

Start Early

No matter where you are financially, today is always a good day to start looking for ways to earn extra and/or passive income. Don't expect to get wealthy through your standard job raises. What can your family really do with a 3% annual increase? On your journey to financial freedom, you have to radically increase your income and/or sources of income. You may have to change your career goals. You may have to step outside of your comfort zone and apply for the top position in your company. You may have to get rid of your cable T.V package, so that you can have some extra funds to invest in a new online business. Are you willing to do what is necessary to increase your income?

Manage Risks

Building wealth is largely about preserving your hard-earned assets. No wealth builder can afford to ignore risk. Risk management is part of everyone's life. One unfortunate event in your life could wipe you out financially. Talking about wealth building is pointless until you have health insurance, because a single medical problem could bankrupt you. Health insurance must become one of your highest priorities. Tens of millions of Americans lack health insurance. Millions more have inadequate coverage. In families with two incomes, one spouse's job usually provides the family with health insurance. If that spouse becomes ill, the job can vanish, along with his or her employer-paid health insurance. If your company doesn't offer it, buy the health insurance yourself. You can search online for information and quotes.

A change in your job can hurt your family financially, if you don't have reserves or other sources of income in place. Most people take action after catastrophe strikes. Don't let this happen to you. You've worked far too hard building up your assets to lose them. *There has never been a better or more important time for YOU to apply the scout motto and 'be prepared'.*

Investing

To be a great investor, be a diligent student. The greatest investment you can make is in yourself! When it comes to investing, a lot of first-time investors want to jump right in with both feet. Regrettably, very few of these investors are successful. Investing in anything requires some degree of skill and knowledge. It is important to remember that few investments are a sure thing - there's the risk of losing your money.

Before you jump right in, it is better to not just try to understand what investing is and how it all works but likewise, to determine what your investment goals are. What do you hope to accomplish with your investments? Will you be funding a college education? Buying a home? Retiring? Before you invest a single dollar, truly consider what you hope to accomplish with that investment. Knowing what your investment goals are will help you make smarter investment decisions along the way!

Too often, people invest their money with dreams of becoming rich overnight. This is possible but rare. It is commonly a bad idea to start investing with hopes of becoming rich overnight. It is safer to invest your cash in such a way that it will grow over time. You ought to strongly consider talking to a financial planner or an experienced investor before making any investments. Your financial advisor may help you determine what type of investment strategy you need to reach your financial goals. They may give you realistic information as to what kind of returns you may expect and how long it will take to reach your particular goals.

Again, remember that investing requires more than calling a financial advisor and telling them that you want to buy stocks or bonds. It takes a certain amount of research and knowledge about the market when you plan to invest successfully. Investing has become increasingly crucial over the years, as the future of social security and company pension plans has become unknown. Naturally, your financial goals will determine what type of investing is right for you. Everyone does not have the same type of financial goals. Don't get caught up in someone else's financial goals, develop your own.

Why Are You Investing?

Two of the primary reasons people invest money is to build wealth and ensure a secure retirement. It is never too early to start investing. Investing is one of the smartest ways to invest in your financial future by putting your money to work. Let me be clear; investing in the stock market may not be for everyone. The key is to identify your financial goals and establish a savings and investment plan. Know what you are saving for and how much you will need to reach your goal. For longer-term objectives, one of the best ways to watch your money grow is to invest it. There are different types of investments you can use to put your money to work. We will get into the different types of investment vehicles further into the chapter.

You may be asking: "how do I begin if I do not have a lot of money to invest?" Contrary to what you may think, investing is not only for people who have an abundance of money; you can get started investing with just a little bit of money and a lot of know-how. But before you do any type of investing, understand what you are getting into. Do your homework before you invest - investigate carefully.

By formulating a plan and familiarizing yourself with the tools available, you can quickly learn how to start investing. Just as you should pay yourself first when you are saving for short-term and long-term goals, you should establish this same habit when investing. The easiest way to do this is by having money automatically deducted from your bank account or paycheck and put into the investment vehicle of your choice. Investing is like driving--it is best done with your eyes wide - open!

Ever heard the saying that goals not written down are just wishes? That applies to your investment goals, too. Having clear-cut reasons or purposes for investing is vital to investing with success. Like conditioning in a fitness center, investing may become tiresome and even risky if you are not working towards a goal and monitoring your progress. Keep in mind that there are always inherent risks associated with investing in most financial market including loss of principal. As with all investment vehicles, your accumulation can increase or decrease, depending on how well the underlying investment perform.

Can You Handle the Risk?

Know your psychological tolerance for financial risk and uncertainty. Understanding your risk tolerance when it comes to investing is all-important to building a portfolio that works well for your hard-earned money. What precisely is investment risk tolerance? Investment risk tolerance defined in general language is the degree of financial loss an investor can handle in reference to major losses in his or her portfolio. The key is to know your own "strengths and weaknesses" as an investor. Don't take too much risk, but don't avoid risk entirely. Safeguard your income and investments. Calculate how much capital you can risk on each investment and outline a worst-case scenario.

You have heard the phrase "don't put all your eggs in one basket." This apply to investing as well. Your risk tolerance is your power, or lack thereof, to take a financial loss. Realizing what kind of risk tolerance, you have is utterly key, and it is something that has to be done prior to you investing your hard-earned money into an investment portfolio, a business or real estate.

How may you find out what sort of risk tolerance you have when it bears on investing? Consider things like your age, income essentials, future financial goals and even your power to control your emotions. An investor who is unable to take many risks at all is said to be risk averse. If you are risk averse, you are likely to invest in assets that protects your principle investment. These are conservative investors.

An investor who is very tolerant of risk tend to be market savvy. They are aggressive in their market approach and they invest in highly volatile instruments. To invest successfully, you must understand the nature of risk posed by different investments.

Before you put your money to work, get to work on knowing what sort of assets you ought to have in your portfolio. This is when you utilize the professional services of a financial advisor. Watching an investment portfolio lose value and being able to sit back and still feel confident about the state of your portfolio is hard to do for many people. Some people are too emotional when it comes to investing in anything where they can lose their money.

You must know yourself and how much risk you are willing to bear. Look at your income needs, your time frame and your tolerance for risk. Be flexible as these things can change as your life changes. Even after you find a suitable investment style, you may need to switch if your financial situation changes drastically.

The investment planning process consists of four vital components which must work together for optimal results. It is important to do a self-assessment of your needs prior to taking any action and the use of a financial specialist is recommended to ensure the process is clear of any emotion. With the proper setup and appropriate dedication to the wealth building plan, it is possible to achieve your objectives in a way that will keep your expenses and stress levels low.

1) Defining Goals and Objectives
a) Purpose for money
b) Time frame for investment
c) Acceptable risk for return

2) Account Type
a) Qualified Account vs. Non-Qualified Account
b) Insured vs. Not-Insured

3) Product Considerations
a) Taxable vs. Not Taxable
b) High Risk vs. Low Risk
c) Liquid vs. Not Liquid
d) High Fees vs. Low Fees

4) Ongoing Management
a) Quarterly review of portfolio

b) Semi-Annual review of plan

c) Annual review of goals and objectives

Know What You Are Getting Into

Never invest in a product, market, or service that you do not fully understand. Your goal is to build wealth and to protect your assets. Wealth is as difficult to preserve as it is to create. There are reasons to invest and there are big reasons why not to invest: debt, a lack of knowledge, and a gamblers mentality. Many people have experienced many sleepless nights because they've gambled with their financial future. They made the mistake of buying investments without any understanding of the risk or regard for what they wanted the investment to do for them.

Speculation is not investing. When it comes to lack of financial knowledge, throwing your money arbitrarily into investments that you do not fully understand is a sure way to lose your money. Investing is a matter of discipline, responsibility and planning. Your reasons for investing are bound to shift as you go through the ups and downs of life. Your reasons and goals will have to be evaluated and adjusted as your conditions changes. Even if nothing important has changed, it is always helpful to reacquaint yourself with your financial goals at regular intervals to see how you have advanced.

Be Careful About Whose Advice You Seek

Financial planning is a process, not a product. Financial professionals are hard to choose, the key is to find someone who understands and is willing to teach you about:

- Investment and asset growth
- Retirement planning
- Taxes

- Estate planning
- Cash management
- Health care cost
- Education funding
- Asset protection

Just as you "carefully" research and select a doctor to take care of your health needs, you need to have just as much consideration when it comes to a financial professional taking care of your money. It is your responsibility and right to fully investigate the advisor's background, methods of practice, credentials, references and other relevant information. You should base your decision for choosing a financial professional on a number of factors:

- What is the planner's education and experience level?
- Does the planner have professional references?
- Can the planner answer technical questions?
- How are you being charged for their services?
- What is the planner's investment beliefs?
- How will they handle your business?
- Is this a short term or long-term relationship?

Typical financial advisor credentials include:
- Certified Financial Planner™ (CFP®)
- Chartered Financial Consultant® (ChFC®)
- Chartered Life Underwriter® (CLU®)
- Personal Financial Specialist (PFS)
- Certified Public Accountant (CPA)
- Registered Financial Consultant (RFC)

When selecting a financial professional, choose one you can work with comfortably. You are paying this person to help guide you during your wealth building years. Don't get caught up in paying any unnecessary fees. You don't build wealth by giving it away. If you feel you are ready to meet with a financial professional, schedule an appointment. Use this opportunity to get a sense of compatibility and to discover exactly how the advisor will work with you.

Ask questions that will give you a basis for a comparison with other financial advisors: How long has the financial advisor been working with clients in the comprehensive financial planning process? What are the advisor's areas of expertise? What type of clientele does the advisor service? It is not uncommon for a financial advisor to work primarily with particular professional groups or income levels. In short, get all the information you need to feel confident that this person is right for you. To work effectively with a personal financial planner, you will need to reveal your personal financial information, so it is important to find someone with whom you feel you can completely trust.

Be suspicious of anyone who tells you, "Invest quickly or you will miss out on a once in a lifetime opportunity." Don't let bogus claims and sales pitches fool you out of your money. Think for yourself; listen to others, but make up your own mind. A wealth builder maintains a long-term investment strategy. Aim to accumulate wealth over time.

Assemble a team of knowledgeable advisers whom you trust. Successfully designing and implementing a wealth building plan is a team effort that involves you, your spouse or significant other, your financial planner, CPA and legal advisors. This team will be there to help you successfully execute your plan.

Creating A Retirement Plan

In these unsure times, investing may be a tool to help you carve out a strong path to retirement. One major reason people do not plan for retirement is that they are too busy with outlandish spending, and overwhelming debts. Some people approaching retirement may lack realistic financial goals for a variety of reasons. Some people cling to unrealistic expectations. Some are procrastinators who don't invest the time to think about retirement's financial challenges.

Everyone has a different notion of what constitutes an ideal retirement. While some may want to travel the world, others volunteer their time to great causes or start their own businesses, while still others just want to relax on a beach. The most important thing to remember is "how much?" – how much cash you need to save to have the retirement you want. The key is to plan a retirement that is meaningful as well as secure.

Though some people want to retire early, others want to work for as long as possible. Whatever your plans for retirement, you need to consider:

1) Are you ready to retire?
2) Will you be single or living with a partner?
3) Will you have adequate health care coverage?
4) What would be your expenses?
5) How should you invest during retirement?
6) Where do you want to live during retirement?

Developing a retirement plan can help ensure that your money will last throughout your retirement years. Many people spend one-third or more of their life in retirement, so it is important to have a plan. One strategy for managing your varying goals is to separate your short-term investment goals from your long-term investment goals.

In general, you will need 65% to 85% of your pre-retirement income to maintain a similar lifestyle in retirement. You want to include all factors such as taxes, real estate cost, health insurance and long-term care.

The more years there are between now and your retirement, the more years your money has time to grow if invested properly. The value of money is an economic concept based on the principles of both investing and inflation. In practical terms, it means that a dollar earned today may be worth more than a dollar earned one year from now. Inflation erodes the purchasing power of money over time. If you do not have a strategy in place to outpace inflation, the less chance there is that you will see any real return on your money.

Types of Retirement Accounts

One of the primary reasons people invest money is to ensure a secure retirement. To make it easier for you to grow your retirement nest egg, the federal government enables you to put your money into certain retirement accounts that have tax advantages. Your retirement plan decisions are extremely important. Today's increased life expectancy means you will spend more years in retirement than previous generations. Be well informed, so you can be well prepared for retirement.

401(k) Plans have proven to be a great investment vehicle for several reasons. The tax deferral is obviously high on this list of reasons. Others include the employer-matching contributions, increased portability and the increased control associated with self-direction of investments. 401k contributions are automatically deducted from an employee's paycheck each pay period. This money is taken out before the paycheck is taxed. The contributions are invested into one or more funds provided by the plan; the employee decides what funds to invest in. Employers often "match" employee contributions but are not required to do so. If your employer is offering matching contributions make sure you take full advantage of it.

403(b) Plans are designed for employees of public schools, colleges and universities, and churches. Employees of certain tax-exempt, non-profit organizations, such as charities and some hospitals, also may participate in a 403(b)-retirement plan – which is also known as a tax-sheltered annuity or tax-deferred annuity. A 403(b)-retirement plan lets you put a portion of your salary into an employer-sponsored plan to help you save for retirement. Some employers may also match your contribution. That is like getting free money for participating in your retirement plan.

A 401(k) or 403(b) plan offers a number of advantages to you. Despite the different names, the plans work similarly. Usually, you decide how much you want taken out of your paycheck to put into your plan. You do not pay taxes on the money you put into the plan. You pay taxes on the money only after you take it out of the plan – usually after you retire. The money you put into the plan usually can be invested in a wide range of investments, from risky to reasonably safe. After you put money into a 401(k) or 403(b) plan, leave it there; the goal is to allow your money to grow. You can borrow from many of these accounts, but borrowing slows down how fast the account grows. If you are younger than 59½ and you are unable to repay the loan you borrowed from your retirement plan, you will pay a penalty 10% on the money you took out.

457 Plans are aimed at state and local government employees of tax-exempt organizations. They work much the same way as 401(k) plans: you can opt to divert part of your salary into the plan and the money is automatically deducted from your paycheck before taxes are taken out. The money grows tax-deferred until it is withdrawn.

Pension Plans are a type of retirement plan, usually tax exempt, wherein an employer makes contributions toward a pool of funds set aside for an employee's future benefit. The pool of funds is then invested on the employee's behalf, allowing the employee to receive benefits upon retirement. In many ways, a pension plan is a method in which an employee transfers part of his or her current income stream towards retirement income. There are two main types of pension plans: defined-benefit plans and defined-contribution plans.

In a defined-benefit plan, the employer guarantees that the employee will receive a definite amount of benefit upon retirement, regardless of the performance of the underlying investment pool. In a defined-contribution plan the employer makes predefined contributions for the employee, but the final amount of benefit received by the employee depends on the investment's performance.

Employee Stock Ownership Plans (ESOP) are used by many companies to compensate, retain and attract employees. These plans are contracts between a company and its employees that give employees the right to buy a specific number of the company's shares at a fixed price within a certain period of time. Employees who are granted stock options hope to profit by exercising their options at a higher price than when they were granted.

Profit Sharing Plans also referred to as a deferred profit-sharing plan, give employees a share in the profits of the company based on the company's earnings.

Annuities are contracts between you and an insurance company in which you make a lump sum payment or series of payments and in return, obtain regular disbursements beginning either immediately or at some point in the future. The goal of annuities is to provide a steady stream of income during retirement. Like 401(k) contributions, annuities can only be withdrawn without penalty after age 59½.

There are several types of Individual Retirement Accounts:

Traditional IRA

The term used to define the regular IRA to participants under age 70½. Annual contributions have a limit of $5,500 ($6,500 if you are age 50 or older). If you are married and your spouse has a job, you and your spouse can put away as much as $11,000 each year ($13,000 if you are both age 50 or older). However, you cannot contribute more than you earned during the year. The money you put into an IRA often can be deducted from your taxable income, so you pay less in taxes each year. You can make a withdrawal from your IRA at any time but there are financial penalties for most early withdrawals— typically, a 10% federal penalty tax and ordinary income tax if you are under age 59½. Under certain conditions, such as buying a home, you may be able to take funds out of certain IRAs without paying a penalty. Earnings on the account are tax deferred until withdrawal, which must begin at age 70½.

Roth IRA

Roth IRAs are similar to traditional IRAs, except that contributions come from after-tax earnings and are not taxed when withdrawn. Annual contributions have a limit of $5,500 ($6,500 if you are age 50 or older). After holding the Roth IRA account for a minimum of five years and/or reaching the age of 59½, all withdrawals are tax-free. The amount of money you can put into a Roth IRA is the same as a traditional IRA; however, you cannot fully fund both. The rules about Roth IRAs are different if you convert money from another account into a Roth IRA. It is best to talk with a tax professional or financial advisor to get the latest information about a Roth IRA.

Simplified Employee Pension (SEP-IRA) – plan provides business owners with a simplified method to contribute toward their employees' retirement as well as their own retirement savings.

Contributions are made to an Individual Retirement Account or Annuity (IRA) set up for each plan participant.

Savings Incentive Matching Plan for Employers IRA (SIMPLE-IRA) – is a retirement plan that may be established by employers, including self-employed individuals. The SIMPLE IRA allows eligible employees to contribute part of their pretax compensation to the plan. The employee contribution limits are: $12,500 ($15,500 for employees age 50 or older).

Types of Investments

Investments are usually made in assets such as stocks, bonds, mutual funds, and real estate. While these types of assets carry more risk than a savings and money market account, they offer the "potential" for you to earn a greater return on your investment. The higher the expected rate of return, the greater the risk. Depending upon market developments, you may lose some or all of your initial investment.

Stock - A type of security that signifies ownership in a corporation and represents a claim on part of the corporation's assets and earnings. There are two main types of stock: common and preferred. Common stock usually entitles the owner to vote at shareholders' meetings and to receive dividends. Preferred stock generally does not have voting rights but has a higher claim on assets and earnings than the common shares. Investing in stocks can be risky. In general, if the company does well, the value of the stock rises and you may receive some of the profits in the form of a dividend. Of course, if the company does not do well, the value of the stock goes down. And you can lose money. There are no guarantees when it comes to investing in stocks.

The stocks you own might be subject to tender offers, mergers, reorganizations or third-party activities that may affect the value of your ownership interest. Securities investments, including mutual funds, are NOT federally insured against a loss in market price.

Bond - A debt investment in which an investor loans money to an entity (corporate or governmental) that borrows the funds for a defined period of time at a fixed interest rate. Bonds are used by companies, municipalities, states, and U.S. and foreign governments to finance a variety of projects and activities. Bonds are commonly referred to as fixed-income securities. Bonds can be divided into two types: taxable and tax-exempt. When you purchase a bond, you are lending money to the issuer. The bond is a legal promise to pay you interest for the use of your money and to repay you the original amount you paid for the bond (the principal). There are various types of risk associated with bonds. The potential for your money to grow, however, is greater than if your money is sitting in a savings account.

Mutual Fund - An investment vehicle that is made up of a pool of funds collected from many investors for the purpose of investing in securities such as stocks, bonds, money market instruments and similar assets. Mutual funds are operated by money managers who invest the fund's capital and attempt to produce capital gains and income for the fund's investors. Investing in mutual funds diversifies your investment so that you do not have all of your eggs in one basket. A mutual fund's portfolio is structured and maintained to match the investment objectives stated in its prospectus.

Diversification: Mutual Funds
Mutual funds are a practical, cost-efficient way to help build a diversified portfolio of investments. Mutual funds can offer built-in diversification and professional management; they offer certain advantages over purchasing individual stocks and bonds. But like

investing in any security, investing in a mutual fund involves certain risks, including the possibility that you may lose money.

Mutual funds provide professional management of your investment. These fund managers have the training and resources to stay abreast of and adjust to market alterations. A successful fund manager has the experience, knowledge and time to seek and track investments—key attributes that you may lack. Regrettably, fund managers do not have a crystal ball presenting them with the ability to foresee the future; do not expect your fund manager to keep you from losing a portion of your investment.

The key is to learn about your investment options and put your funds in the best place for you, - stocks, insurance, IRAs, annuities or other financial alternatives. You can learn about the world of finance by reading publications on the subject, such as Barron's and Fortune. Continue to study the financial market, there is always more you can learn and apply as the economy changes.

Real Estate as Investment
Real estate investing can be a very profitable business if handled properly. Real estate is at the core of almost every business, and it's certainly at the core of most people's wealth. Real estate is one of the most profitable types of investments because of the need for housing and business locations. Property prices are affected by the market and can drop, but smart investors know that property rarely goes down in value and if it does, it usually rebounds.

Some people buy a property and then sell it for profit and some people will take that same property and rent it out for cash flow. These people are called real estate investors. Investing in real estate has numerous tax advantages, particularly because you are allowed to use depreciation to offset the income you receive from a property.

There are many strategies that can be used when it comes to real estate investing.

Residential Real Estate

Investment in residential real estate is the most common form of real estate investment. Properties such as single-family homes, apartment buildings, townhouses, and vacation homes where people pay you to live in the property is great for creating cash flow. The key to being successful in residential real estate investing is to know your numbers. Investing in a property that has not been properly inspected can cost you or either wipe you out financially.

Commercial Real Estate

Commercial real estate consists of office buildings, retail space (shopping malls, strip malls, and storefront properties), skyscrapers, hotels and motels, warehouses and other commercial properties. When you get into investing in commercial real estate, you are playing on a whole different level. The commercial real estate investment business is a very small competitive market, because not many people have the knowledge or capital to invest in these types of ventures.

Any experienced real estate investor will tell you, not all investment properties are created equal. You must do your homework if you plan to get into real estate investing. It is a great strategy for building wealth, if you have a long-term vision. The key criteria in these investments that we focus on is that they are income producing.

The Right Frame of Mind: *Don't be a backseat driver.*

Every plan you make and every action you take, is an investment in your future – whether for wealth, knowledge, health, relationships, financial freedom, or any long-term goal. The most important part of having a plan is implementing it. No one is going to take the wheel and drive you towards your goals. You have to take responsibility for your own fate and be prepared to take action to accomplish it.

When an opportunity comes your way that fits into your financial goal and you have done all your research and discussed it over with your team, do not allow yourself to get paralyzed by fear and lapse into inactivity. A lot of fears are irrational when it comes to investing and by listening to them, you tend to procrastinate.

Early in my investment career, I was presented with an opportunity to invest in the early stages of a company we all know as Google, but I passed on the opportunity. I did not have a full understanding of the company, and my doubts prevented me from stepping out of my comfort zone. All investors feel nervous at some point or another. When I look at the performance of the company, investing in Google at that time would have been a great opportunity for my business. It is one of those "Only if I" moments in my life.

Activate Wealth Building Principles. Do not allow fear to cloud your determination to become financially free. Buy assets that will provide you with cash flow instead of purchasing liabilities. No matter what you aspire to, how you use the time and money you have will determine whether you make your wealth building future a reality, or whether it will exist only as an unfulfilled dream. Save and invest your money.

The Science of Being a Wealth Builder

Increase your sources of income and save at least 20% of your net pay every pay period. Never live on 100% of your income. Do not be one paycheck away from financial havoc.

Invest your savings. Put your money to work for you. Increase your knowledge, expertise and skills, so you can earn more money. Gain financial wealth building wisdom and take action. Read financial publications such as the Wall Street Journal, New York Times, Forbes, Money magazine, etc. *Re-read this book once a quarter.*

Before you make a purchase, ask yourself: "Is this a "want" or a "need?" Do not spend on needless things. Little expenses for seemingly insignificant purchases add up to large sums over time. You may not always make the right decision, but at least take the time to think before you make a purchase.

Have a financial purpose plan. Always have a long-term goal for your money. Save and invest your money with a purpose, whether it is to buy a house, investment properties, a business or retirement income. When your money has a purpose, you can live the life YOU want.

INVESTOR
ECONOMY
GROWTH
CURRENCY
COMPANIES
FINANCIAL
WEALTH
MONEY
PLAN
BUSINESS
PROFIT
BANK
MARKET
CONCEPT
DIAGRAM
INVESTMENT
FINANCE
CHART
CORPORATE
PROPERTY
GROUP
ASSET
COIN
GRAPH
MALE
INCOME
PROGRESS
ENTERPRISE
CONNECTION
PRICE
REPORT
INFORMATION
SUCCESS
BENEFIT
SYMBOL
SCREEN
GRAPHIC
EURO
RISE
DIGITAL
CLOUD
GROWING
ARROW
RISK
IDEA
BUSINESSMAN
HOUSE
TRADE
HUMAN
SHARES
GOAL
FIGURES
EARNINGS
FUND
CAPITAL
DESIGN
MANAGER
RATE
PERSON
STATISTICS
COMPANY
ANALYSIS
GAIN
HAND
BANKING
HOME
FIRM
GLOBAL
PROFESSIONAL
CONSTRUCTION
ACCOUNTING
DEVELOPMENT
MANAGEMENT
DATA

"Wealth is the product of energy times intelligence: energy turned into artifacts that "advantage" human life." - Buckminster Fuller

CHAPTER III
WEALTH IS NOT A DESTINATION BUT A JOURNEY

Begin every journey by starting with the end. If you clearly understand where you want to be, you can make sure that your actions each and every day will bring you one step closer to that desired place. Many people believe that "money" is the key factor that separates financially successful people from financially unsuccessful people. In most instances, however, the missing factors are financial literacy and a financial plan. I know a lot of people who have "money" but they don't know what to do with it. All they do is earn and spend. Earning is cool, but the key is to know how to manage it, grow it, and invest it. **True financial wealth is a collection of assets, not liabilities.** Developing the habit of saving and investing your money is not easy.

The key to success is self-discipline. Doing what needs to be done instead of what you want to do is the essence of self-discipline. You need to take responsibility for yourself. You and you alone have the power to fulfill your financial goals. It requires determination and focus. By practicing "self-control," you will like yourself more. You'll feel a sense of pride and accomplishment, and enjoy an enhanced self-image. Ultimately, you'll feel empowered, in charge and positive about the future.

You can improve your financial skills through training, information and guidance. Such financial education can help you better understand "financial products, concepts and risks." Your consistent investment in your financial education will increase your confidence in your ability to make financial decisions and choices. Financially literate people understand the wealth building process of budgeting, saving money, controlling spending, handling debt, planning for retirement, and participating in financial markets.

Today, many people function in an 'instant' mentality; they want everything instantly. Some so-called gurus may tell you that you can quantum leap to financial freedom but my friend, it just does not work that way. The internet abounds with schemes offering you millions of dollars for basically sitting on your backside. Wealthy people find all this very amusing. The only one making money from those scams is the person processing your credit card or cashing your check. It requires work to build wealth, and 90 percent of the work is on your thinking, attitude and beliefs about money. Before you can see a change in your finances, you first have to change your thinking. There are no shortcuts to success.

From the earlier stages in my life, I was taught that I had to work hard and trade my time for money. But I was never taught how to have my money work smart for me to make me more money. I had to make the choice to go on this journey of building wealth. There are two kinds of people in the world, those who make things happen and those who complain about what's happening. The biggest and greatest investment I've ever made was in myself. I know there is a 100% guarantee that nothing will change unless I do. I can earn a million dollars and know what to do with it because I've studied and applied principles of wealth.

You must give yourself permission to be wealthy. You have to set a financial goal, write it down, make a plan and consistently work on it all the time. The more clearly your vision for financial freedom is, the closer you will move towards it and the closer it will move towards you.

You must learn to take control and apply the principles that are necessary to become a wealth builder. When you begin living from your new money mindset, you start to make different decisions. You begin to associate with different kinds of people and you attract different circumstances into your life.

"Success is a matter of understanding and religiously practicing specific, simple habits that always lead to success." **Robert J. Ringer**

Warning: There will always be those who say that something cannot be done or worse, that you cannot do it. Fulfilling your desire of being a wealth builder requires an unwavering commitment to a goal that cannot be shaken by the negative uneducated comments of others. You cannot let others limit your thinking in what you desire to accomplish or what you can do.

Learn "the language of economics" and work to understand strategy, planning and finance. You must realize that other people can program you with their limiting thinking, so when people say things to you that are less than what you want, make a mental note that it is their opinion and not what is true. People will try to tell you what you qualify for and your level of ability. **No one can take your power, unless YOU give them full authorization to control your mind.** There are four things that never return: the spoken word, the speeding arrow, the wasted life, and the neglected opportunity. You can lead someone to knowledge, but you cannot make them THINK.

"Whoever walks with the wise becomes wise, but the companion of fools will suffer harm." **Proverbs 13:20, ESV**

You must, at all cost, watch who you allow into your trusted circle of friends. By default, most people dwell on the negative – what they do not want to have happen – as opposed to the good things that could happen. This habit springs from social conditioning and past experiences. It does not take long after you have decided to become a wealth builder that you begin to realize that your old friends whom you have known for years start to treat you differently, especially if you were the friend who always paid for everything. They begin to see the changes in you and for some, they feel uncomfortable with your new-found money habits.

How would it affect you when you see that trusted friends no longer want to be around you as they once did? Disappointed a little? Of course. This is the reality of coming into a brand-new way of living financially; you find some of your friends are going to change. This is where many give up on the financial journey because they are afraid of losing what they considered a genuine relationship. I have news for you: if a person does not want to be around you because you've made a positive change in your life and you are no longer spending money on them, then that is NOT a real friendship. Many will be a distraction and you will have to limit your time with them as you travel on your financial journey.

Don't settle for mediocrity - Change! Either do nothing and let change happen to you, or find opportunities to make change work for you. It's your choice. Change affects your routine and your attitude.

Successful people don't succumb to procrastination or temporary distractions. Financial freedom is within the reach of anyone who has a burning desire to achieve it. You must be persistent and consistent in developing the habits of those who are already successful. However, it will not be easy; it will require some major adjustments in your thinking, beliefs and attitudes about money. For example, when my business partners and I first built our investment business, in the beginning stages as a company, we were strapped for cash. Any cash flow we received was reinvested back into the business, and we knew that all the sacrifices we made were going to pay off. All of the executives, including myself, did not take a salary for the first two years.

Our desire for building a successful company was much greater than our short-term cash flow circumstances. We knew what we wanted, we created the vision, we developed the plan and we took action. All these things are important but if we did not have the desire that was strong enough to get us through those rough periods, we would have given up in the earlier stages. Goals, action plans, and outcomes are worthless without proper motivation.

There is nothing in life that can defeat you or deny you of success but yourself. Your own limiting thinking can defeat you; your lack of determination, indecisiveness and lack of confidence in yourself can defeat you but only if you let these negative attributes take hold. Pessimism is a learned behavior that can be changed. You have the power to change your conditions. Believe in yourself. Allow positive thinking to dominate your thoughts. Your success in life is up to you. Success will only come when you believe you deserve it. - **"According to your faith be it unto you."** **Matthew 9:29**

If you want to be wealthy, redirect the energy you put into making excuses for your financial setbacks, into making progress. **YOU are your most valuable asset.** By investing in your craft and developing your skills, you increase your worth and earnings potential. However, you need to commit to making this a priority throughout your life and wealth building journey. It is up to you to be all that you want to be, to do all that you want to do and to have all that you want to have. Life is about being, doing and having.

You are in charge. Think of your life as a movie. You are the writer, director, producer and star. You choose who gets to play a role in your movie. Whether the movie is a financial box office hit or a flop, it is in your hands. Your thoughts determine your outcome. If you think you are average, you are. If you think you cannot win, you will not. Conversely, if you see yourself succeeding, you will. If you expect great things to come into your life, they are on their way. When you lift yourself up, you lift up those close to you, too. The first and most important rule is to take responsibility for everything that happens in your life. Following this rule puts you in charge. Are you ready to command your future?

The key to living your life to the fullest is to never allow money to determine what you can and cannot do. Do not limit yourself and never allow a dollar to limit you either. Do not let your traditional thinking close your mind and prevent you from seeing the real truth: God wants YOU to prosper. God wants YOU to abound, and it is His blessing that enables YOU to accumulate wealth. God's basic desire for us is that we grow beyond simply being blessed and become a blessing to others.

"Beloved, I wish above all things that thou mayest prosper and be in health, even as thy soul prospereth." **3 John 2**

The accumulation of wealth is not a destination, but a journey. The people who have achieved financial freedom have paid the price on their journey. They stayed the course when others may have given up. Those who succeed in life commit to doing what they love and money will follow. Financial success is not going to be handed to you; you have to challenge any self-defeating beliefs and take massive action. **How you think about money and what you believe tend to materialize in your life.** It is time to become a wealth builder. If you want the same results as the wealthy, then you must take the necessary actions to create those results.

THE 10 CASH ONLY COMMANDMENTS OF MONEY

COMMANDMENT I

Know Thy Source. Remember the LORD your God, for it is he who gives YOU the ability to produce wealth. When you are elevated financially, remember where your blessings come from. Avoid arrogance and be humble and grateful for the blessings God has bestowed upon you. Do not put your trust in money, but in the living God. *"The blessing of the Lord, it maketh rich, and he added no sorrow with it."* **Proverbs 10:22** God is the source of your abundance. God has laid down a firm foundational plan to teach you how to become rich without sorrows. Keep in mind that these are God's words, not ours. **God is the source, YOU are the asset and money is the servant.** Never put a servant in the place of a master. God must come before money. If you spend five minutes a day seeking God's wisdom and eight hours a day chasing after money, then who or (what) is your source?

It is a matter of priority. Invest in your spiritual health to attain inner peace. Discipline yourself to separate your emotions from material things. God does not want to deprive you of the things you need to live, and to live abundantly. He just wants you to remember He is the source of it all. When you begin to experience the prosperous life, do not stop seeking God. As surely as you do, those things that God so richly blessed you with will begin to fall away. Part of your continuing success depends upon your recognition that God is your source. God is the one who supplies everything you need. With every upward advance in your wealth, learn to express gratitude. Give honor to God for the abundant harvest you are receiving.

COMMANDMENT II

Master Thy Servant (Money). **Never allow money to decide what you can and cannot do**. The first place to master money is in your mind. Wealth is created mentally first; it is thought out before it becomes a reality. God has established certain principles of economics that govern who will be wealthy and who will be poor. If we follow the principles that lead to wealth, we will be wealthy. We all play an important part in determining our own financial situations.

Never allow money to determine what you can and cannot do. If you think too much about the lack of money or too much about your debt, all these things will tend to bring to you the very thing you are attempting to get away from. You can attract the things you desire as easily as you can attract the thing you hate and despise and long to get rid of. You can only rise and conquer your finances by lifting up your thoughts.

When you operate the wealth builder's principles in your life, you will begin to experience abundance and become the master of money.

COMMANDMENT III

Have a Storehouse to Manage Your Money. In order to manage your money, you need a storehouse. Carefully selecting a financial institution is probably the most important part of the process because selecting a bank that is a bad fit could mean you have to start your search all over again in a few months. That search should start with looking at what your priorities are for a checking, savings and investment account. By knowing the cost and requirements for each of your accounts, it can save you the hassle and avoid unexpected fees. Every day we see various financial institutions waging war with their competitors. They try to offer us some incentive that will convince us to deposit our money with their bank. Some offer higher interest rates on money market accounts. Others offer free checking accounts with online banking. This is all nice, but you want to build a relationship with a financial institution that values you as a client.

COMMANDMENT IV

Know Thy Assets and Liabilities. Assets increase in value, liabilities decrease in value. An asset puts money into your pocket; an asset should increase in value. Liabilities are the opposite of assets. Liabilities take money out of your pocket. Work to increase your assets and decrease your liabilities. Know the difference between good and bad debt.

What is good debt? When you use OPM (other people's money) to invest in an asset that provides a cash flow to pay back the debt, puts money in your pocket, and appreciates in value. These forms of debt "usually" have low interest rates and therefore can be maintained for long periods of time as you build up your assets. Bad debt includes debt you have taken on for things you do not need or cannot afford that decrease in value. The worst form of bad debt is consumer credit cards since they usually carry the highest interest rates. Interest rates for credit cards can far exceed even the best investments which would negatively impact your overall cash flow. Most people get into money trouble because they don't exercise self-control. They want immediate gratification; they equate happiness with acquisition.

COMMANDMENT V

Know Where Thy CASH Flows. Measure your cash flow by tracking your weekly and monthly expenses versus your weekly and monthly income. Review your monthly bank statements, know where your cash is coming from and going to. Take advantage of a number of services offered by your bank, including direct deposit and automatic bill pay. Make the most of online banking. To make the tracking of your expenses easy and accurate, pay for all your household expenses using one dedicated checking account. Grow your income more quickly than your expenses, so that each year you can devote more resources towards your long-term financial goals.

COMMANDMENT VI

Learn From Thy Fellow Money Masters. Seek out a mentor, someone who has already mastered money. Having mentors who have achieved success in their life is important to your success. Many have already traveled the road you may be on. I remember the advice from my mentor was: "Always learn from other people's mistakes and successes. It will save you time and money." Learn from those who have what you want; be a student of the financial game. Consider joining with other money masters either in an internet community (CASH ONLY Online Community) or in a physical community. Others with a similar mindset as your own can go a long way when it comes to helping you learn new financial skills, building your financial strengths, and identifying and overcoming your weaknesses. Read investing books, read the annual reports of the companies in your portfolio, and pay close attention to the news on the economy.

COMMANDMENT VII

Know Thy Friends. Do not waste your time discussing finances with someone who is not supportive of your financial education. You must stand on guard at the door of your thoughts; keep out all the enemies of your happiness and achievement. **"The less you associate with some people, the more your life will improve. Any time you tolerate mediocrity in others, it increases your mediocrity."** Colin Powell

We get so comfortable talking to the same individuals inside our circle of friends that we do not realize that how much we hear only supports our biases. Develop and expand your network; learn from those who are in position to help you achieve your goals. If you are not willing to learn, no one can help you. If you are determined to learn, no one can stop you. Build relationships with people who can help you grow, but don't be selfish, you must bring something to the table as well.

You cannot grow as long as you divide your loyalties with people, places and things that do not add-value to your life's mission.

COMMANDMENT VIII

Multiply Thy Streams of Income. Do not rely on one stream of income; if that one stream dries up, it can put you in a financial bind. Creating multiple streams of income ensures you will always be earning income. Creating multiple streams of income requires time, education, consistent work and commitment. If you want to earn more, work less and have financial freedom, you are going to have to start creating multiple income streams that do not require too much of your time. Release the traditional thinking of a "safe and secure job" and "playing it safe" behaviors. You will not be able to see the opportunities around you that could be a potential stream of income unless you are willing to learn from everything around you. Go to where the growth is and where you are able to bring in revenue. Do not chase after just any business; choose the business where you are able to grow and profit. You will gain financial freedom as well as time freedom.

COMMANDMENT IX

Owe No Man. The rich rule over the poor, and the borrower is servant to the lender. When you develop the habit of always borrowing money, you can be known as a leech. By having too much debt, it limits your chances of taking advantage of investment opportunities. Get intense, do away with your debt so that you may be free of those interest payments and start investing your money on the things that matter as you save for your future.

COMMANDMENT X

Spread the Wealth. Anything you hoard and keep that should be shared becomes your god. When you are generous and you spread your wealth to worthy causes, your giving allows God the opportunity to bless you and to give you more than enough. By your faithful obedience in your giving, you set into motion God's principles of biblical economics. *"A man's gift maketh room for him, and bringeth him before great men."* **Proverbs 18:16**

When we are wealthy, our blessing is to be a blessing to others. You can never consider yourself wealthy if you do not have the heart to be generous with your money. As you give, so shall you receive. If you do not sow, you cannot reap. To have wealth in abundance, you must first begin to give, creating a new, life-changing flow to your wealth. Stagnant wealth cannot draw new wealth to you. Giving and receiving are interrelated and interdependent upon each other.

Stay focused as you continue on this journey of wealth building. There will be distractions. Things will get in the way. You will have excuses, but none of them will help you.

"Your net worth to the world is usually determined by what remains after your bad habits are subtracted from your good ones." - Benjamin Franklin

CHAPTER IV
THE WISDOM OF WEALTH

Many people misunderstand the idea of being wealthy. Many "try" to get rich by their own will power and human ingenuity. They gather up riches for themselves but make a grave mistake of leaving out the most important things in life: they neglect their spiritual life, family and health. What is the point of wealth without health? **"Without health, you will not enjoy your wealth."** What purpose is there to have all the wealth you desire but you do not have the health to enjoy it? Taking control of your health is of utmost importance because your mind and body are your most valuable assets. Do not let your net worth take your self-worth. **Your true wealth is priceless.**

Your beliefs about what you are worth and how money plays into that equation have a huge impact on how you build wealth. Financial success reflects only a small piece of the bigger picture that is your life. You could have all the money in the world but if you do not have peace, or someone special to share it with, then it would be senseless. When the benchmark for your happiness is material things, you can live constantly in a state of bondage. Wealth building is about freeing yourself to live a complete life and manifest your full capabilities, which can include making a real contribution to the welfare of others.

Life could be lonely without good people to experience it with. I just realized something: Benjamin Franklin, Andrew Jackson, Abraham Lincoln, or George Washington (figure heads on money) never hugged me in the middle of the night. It would be scary if they did, but you know what I mean. When my wife and I started out on the journey of wealth building we made a commitment to make sure we took the time out to focus on the things that mattered to our family. Even though our schedules were hectic from running our businesses, we made it a priority to go on dates and take family trips. Too many couples are torn apart over a power struggle rooted in money and materialism.

Money simply does not guarantee happiness, but it also does not mean that you can neglect your financial responsibilities and live your life like a pauper. True happiness and lasting peace comes from your relationship with your Creator, taking care of your mental state, and providing for your family. When you have your priorities in order, your journey of wealth building will not cause you to neglect the important people and things in your life.

Many make decisions in their pursuit for money that seem right but turn out to be deadly. Money must be put in its proper place as a servant, not a master. I love this quote by writer George Lorimer: **"It is good to have money and the things that money can buy, but it is good, too, to check up once in a while and make sure that you have not lost the things that money cannot buy."** Money can master us or we can master it.

We all must learn how to master money rather than be enslaved by it. Money can do many good things but when it is not controlled, it can literally destroy us. How we utilize our money has a bigger influence on our happiness than how much money we have. When you have the right attitude about the use of money, you can do good in this world.

Peace, power and prosperity are found within YOU, not money. Money is a good tool if used properly. Money is to be regarded as a servant that comes to help and assist your life for prosperous living.

It is important to start shifting your mentality about money. In essence, if you think of money with the right thoughts, you will master money. On the other hand, if you are always worried about money, or even subconsciously reject the idea of having money or think there is something wrong with wanting or believing that you deserve money, then you are pushing money away from you. Money is whatever you want it to be, you give money its meaning.

"Cash is far more powerful in the hands of someone who knows how to invest it wisely, than someone who spends every dollar that touches their hand. Most people would not know what to do with a million dollars, other than spend it." - CASH ONLY Strategist

Confront your own feelings about money. Many are unaware of the wealth that is available to them. Some believe they do not deserve to have wealth. Then there are those who believe that to deny oneself of wealth is noble. There is nothing noble about living in lack, not knowing how you are going to pay your bills or feed your family. Go tell someone who is unable to provide for their family that it is noble for their children to be hungry. Make sure you run after you make that statement. Traditional erroneous thinking has some people believing that God does not want His children to be wealthy. I never subscribed to that way of thinking and I advise you not to, as well.

The 9 Money Languages

What Money Language Do You Currently Speak?

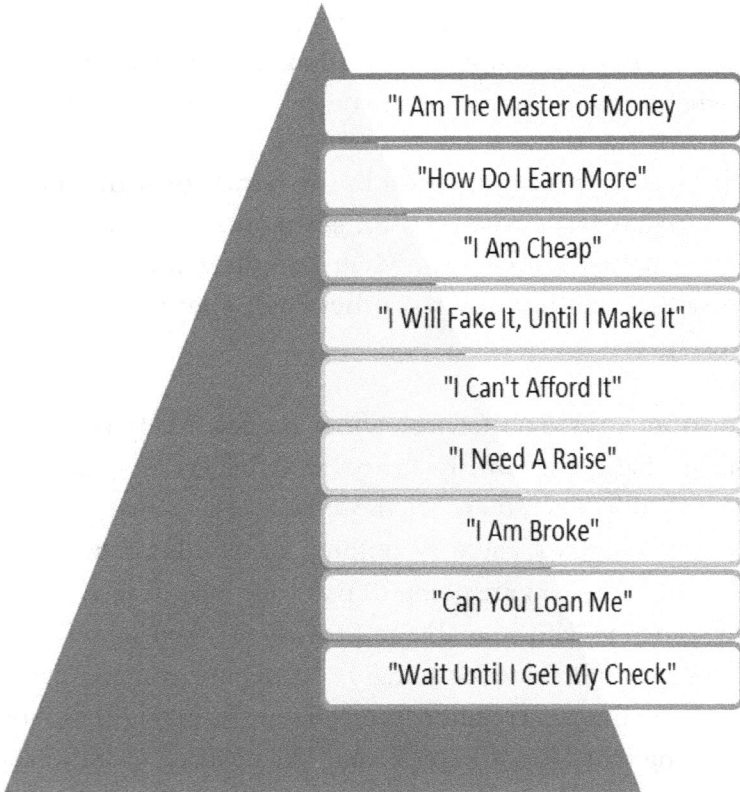

"I Am The Master of Money

"How Do I Earn More"

"I Am Cheap"

"I Will Fake It, Until I Make It"

"I Can't Afford It"

"I Need A Raise"

"I Am Broke"

"Can You Loan Me"

"Wait Until I Get My Check"

Money Languages: What Language Do You Speak?

Our money language is passed down from generation to generation. We learn the language of money by what we hear from our parents, friends, teachers, religious beliefs, musical influences and everything in our environment. Think back to the phrases that you heard as a child. What do you recall? Phrases such as, "that is too expensive," "we cannot afford that" and other similar utterances may be familiar to many people. Your memories about money will tell you a great deal about how you were influenced by those around you and whether those memories still influence how you handle money today.

When it comes to talking about money, most people feel shame, guilt, abandonment and fear – usually based on experiences from their childhood. With money, you determine the language you want to speak; and if you do not like the money language you currently speak, you can always learn a new one. There are no limits to your ability to think and change your financial habits.

"Wait Until I Get My Check" This money language is spoken by those who always seem to have to wait until they receive a paycheck to make any kind of purchase. When you hear "Wait until I get my check," you know what money language this person speaks. We call this the living from paycheck to paycheck language of money. We all may have started out from this position at one point in our careers. I recall when I was working as a security guard, my mindset at that time was a paycheck mindset. I only made enough income to get to and from work. My friends would ask me to go out with them on weekend vacations but at that time, I did not have the discipline to save money.

I barely was able to pay my monthly obligations. I developed the habit of speaking the money language of "Wait until I get my paycheck." It was a struggle to break this money language. I had to change my financial habits. I had to learn to set aside a portion of my income, despite the circumstances of not earning enough. In order to break free from the paycheck to paycheck lifestyle, one must become sick and tired of being sick and tired of this lifestyle. Until this money language becomes uncomfortable, people will continue to live the life as an underearner.

How do I change my "wait until I get my check" money language? You first must change the way you think about money. What type of relationship do you have with your money? Is it an appreciative relationship or are you frustrated by your lack of it? As you learn more about your money beliefs, you will gain more of an understanding about your money habits.

Create a list of your financial priorities. Begin tracking all of your spending on a daily basis; know where thy cash is flowing. Begin to use cash or your debit card instead of using your credit card. The key is to not accumulate any debt and to know what you are spending your money on. Change your thinking so that saving cash becomes a source of satisfaction. As your savings grow, you'll have funds to invest in income producing opportunities.

Saving at least 20% of your paycheck is fundamental to breaking the cycle of living paycheck to paycheck because you are putting yourself in a position to build wealth. You must make paying yourself first a priority. You can make your first payment from your earnings in the form of an automatic deposit to your wealth building account.

"Can You Loan Me?" Although, some people are responsible enough to pay back what they borrow, some are habitual borrowers. This money language is spoken by those who are always looking for a hand out. Always taking and never giving. They promise to pay you back, but you can never find them or hear from them until they need to borrow again. We call this the borrower's language of money.

You probably have some people in your life at this moment you know who speak this money language. These people are always asking for loans and know how to manipulate others. They make people feel guilty when they tell them "no." Excuses are all these people make for not having any money. It requires work to break a beggar's mentality.

A strong accountability group is needed, because people who speak this money language look for people who enable them, and they can easily take advantage of. If you speak the "Can you loan me?" money language and many will deny it, know that your mentality is a hindrance to you experiencing true financial freedom.

How do I change my "Can you loan me?" money language? First, call everyone that you owe money to and tell them that you have decided to pay back all you have borrowed. Don't just "say" you're going to repay them, actually make the effort and do it. So, list all of your debt obligations and arrange them in order from the smallest balance to the largest. Begin with the smallest balance by putting as much as you can above and beyond the minimal amount toward your payment.

When you finish paying off the debt, then celebrate! Celebrate the fact that you are no longer a slave to your lender. **"The rich rule over the poor, and the borrower is slave to the lender."** Proverbs 22:7 You have now elevated from "Can you loan me?" to freedom. You've gained back your power. This is an awesome way to move your mindset from personally being helped to putting away a portion of your income to help and empower others.

When you change your mindset from helping "Me and mines and no more" to "My giving will be changing the future of generations to come," you have now elevated your language of money and your use of money. You have now risen to putting your money and yourself in the position of inspiration.

"I Am Broke" Being broke is not a pleasant experience. The morale of a person who is always broke is one that is fragile. Their insecurity regarding finances is brought to light during financial conversations. People who speak the "I Am Broke" money language claim to never have any money but always seem to be buying things. They spend a great deal of time at the local malls shopping, yet never have any money to save. We call this the broke person's mentality of money.

Being broke is a temporary state of being. In my earlier working years, I lived in this temporary state of being broke for a while. No matter how hard I worked, it always seemed that I did not have enough money. I heard the older folks say: "The harder you work, the more you make." I am not saying they did not know what they were talking about, but this type of advice did not work for me. I worked from 8 until faint and still, my bank account had the same $3.00 at the end of the month.

How do I change my "I am broke" money language?

When I started to work smart and save my money, I began to see a change in my finances. I first created a tracking sheet to see where my money was going, because it sure was not going into my bank account. I noticed that I was spending a large portion of my income on eating at restaurants while I was at work. The harder I worked, the hungrier I got and the more I spent my money.

To rectify my use of money, I shifted my spending habits at work. Instead of buying lunch, I brought my lunch from home. Let me be honest here… my wife forced me into eating leftovers and it paid off. I went from being broke to having a surplus; I was saving an additional $500 a month just by eating leftovers. So, at the end of the month, there was $503 in the account to go towards saving and investing. My financially-disciplined life paid off and is still serving me well to this day.

"I Need A Raise" This is the "needy" money language; this individual is always expecting something. They also believe more money is going to solve their money problems. They believe that by trading more of their time, they should receive more money. Now consider this: the average annual pay raise is about 0.5-2%. Is your time worth more than 0.5%? I am not advising you to deny yourself a raise or not accept it.

My advice to you is to never allow a raise to suppress the creative spirit in you. There is a creative idea on the inside of you that can yield more income than that raise you are seeking. When I was working, I used to think that a raise would help me. Yet when they gave me that raise of $1.50, I would just get upset. I would have to work much harder for that $1.50 and inevitably, the cost of living would go up and I ended up back where I started in terms of my income not being able to meet the needs of my expenses.

How do I change my "I need a raise" money language? When you settle for a job that you dislike, you suppress or exchange your creativity for a paycheck. You can get trapped into the idea of always looking forward to your next annual 2% pay raise and missing your creative voice telling you that you can do better or be earning more by doing something that you enjoy. Do what you love and you'll never work another day in your life. **Always give yourself a raise because no one else will ever give you the raise you deserve**. If you are creative, look for ways you can increase your income. Make a list of things you can do that can provide some extra income and not require a great deal of your time. For example, if your spouse has asked you to clean the cluttered garage for the past two years, use this opportunity to have a garage sale.

"I Can't Afford It" This money language is spoken by those who know the price of everything and yet are unable to determine the value of anything. This person allows money to determine what they can and cannot do. Instead of creatively devising a way to attain the money needed to buy the item, this person would rather put it out of their mind all together. **This person knows what they want and yet automatically feels like they do not deserve it**. They place too much value on the price instead of what they want. It almost seems like they have thoughts of unworthiness. They are the only one who can change these kind of limiting beliefs and come to a sense of worthiness within.

How can I change my "I can't afford it" money language?
When you ask yourself, "How Can I Afford It?" you are now setting your mind in motion to make your dream of attainment become reality. I am not advocating going out to purchase items that have no value, like clothes that you wear one time or hang in your closet with the tag on. Rather, I am promoting that you open your mind to the possibilities of attaining assets that will add to your wealth and have some form of resale value. The point is to ask yourself: "How can I afford it?" and then, "What is my plan of action after I attain it?"

"I Will Fake It Until I Make It" This may surprise you that this is a money language. You have many financial gurus who say the best way to make yourself believe that you are rich is to fake it until you make it. These individuals are the best dressed at every social gathering. They buy expensive items on credit. They look good and smell good but owe everybody. You look inside their closets and they have a closet full of knock off products. Their watch is supposed to be a Rolex but since it is an imitation: it says Nolex. Do not fake it! Be authentic!

How can I change my "I will fake it until I make it" money language? If you purchase fake products to appear rich, you are doing yourself a disservice. By being fake, you are not being true to yourself. You are more concerned about what people think of you. If this is you, I encourage you to live authentically. You do not need to impress anyone but yourself. This act of courage on your part will show that you have self-respect. **It is good to wait until you have**

more than enough cash flow and you have your financial house in order so that you may be able to purchase the real thing. Being authentic is the only way to live!

When I first learned about dressing for success, I asked some successful business men about different types of suits, and the best advice I got was, "do not buy cheap suits." Did I listen? No. At that time I did not believe I should be spending more than $69.00 for a suit. Do not laugh, yes, you read it right, $69.00 for suit. I thought I was hot stuff in my $69.00 polyester suit.

I wore that suit until it was out of style. I probably would have kept that suit until that infamous day. This was my only suit at the time, so needless to say I wore it a lot. Well one day as I was preparing to put on that suit, I stood in front of the mirror to check how good I looked. It was a beautiful day and the sun was shining, when I looked in the mirror I noticed my suit had iron prints all over it, from me ironing it every week. This was my first lesson in clothing: do not buy cheap polyester suits. Polyester wears faster, and produces shiny spots. Now I know why people were laughing at me when they saw me in that suit. (Pardon me, I just had another flashback.) Do you think after this experience I listened to the businessmen who told me to buy an all-wool suit? Absolutely...not.

I was in the business of being conservative with my money (cheap), I was watching my cash flow, and so I went out and brought not one, but two $79.00 polyester suits. I thought I was like Ervin Magic Johnson with the $10.00 increase in my suit purchase, styling and profiling. Did things change because I spent $10.00 more on the suits? Oh no, I just ended up with two cheap polyester suits with iron prints on them. Take it from me, it may cost more for all wool suits, but it is well worth the investment. Also, you do not look prosperous walking around with a cheap polyester suit with shiny iron prints on it. You will never get a second chance to make a first impression.

Evaluate yourself to determine if you are presenting yourself in the best light. Take an objective look. Does your look and dress portray success? Maybe it is time for a make-over and not a $69.00 makeover. When you look good, you will feel better about yourself and your attitude will exude confidence. Confidence attracts success, and believe me, you cannot be confident walking around with a polyester suit with iron prints all over it. **Key: Don't fake it and purchase cheap items.**

"I Am Cheap" This money language is spoken by those who may have money but are too scared to part with it. Being cheap has nothing to do with how much money you have. You can be rich and cheap, or broke and cheap. People who are cheap buy everything at the second-hand stores and spend hours of the day clipping coupons in efforts to hoard their money. They are the ones who run to the bathroom when the bill comes when you are at the restaurant or they will pull out their calculator and start crunching numbers on their portion of the meal. Let me make this clear: there is nothing wrong in clipping coupons to get extra savings or a discount. Give me a pair of scissors and some coupons I will be clipping to save those dollars. The "I Am Cheap" mentality/language becomes a problem when the ultimate result is the hoarding of money.

How do I change my "I am cheap" money language? As stated earlier in this book, much of the money language habits are learned from childhood. If you speak and live the "I Am Cheap" money language, it may be because you were a person who may have grown up poor and did not have much. Then when you began to earn money, you were constantly reminding yourself of when you had to do without because of the lack of money. You end up placing a great deal of value on money; you believe the money is going to save you from poverty when poverty has more to do with a mindset. You must forgive your past, realizing that the past is not the present and does not equal the future. Make a choice to enjoy your life. Be smart, not cheap. Enjoy your money before you leave this earth because if you don't, someone else is going to enjoy spending your money doing fun things.

"How Can I Earn More?" This money language is spoken by the creators in society. This group develop plans to earn money; they are not looking for handouts. They earn money and continue the process of earning more money through their creative use of ideas. They are always looking for opportunities and ways to add value and solve the problems of the masses. If the person is not satisfied with their current income they look for opportunities to expand, either through creative ideas or business opportunities.

The creators in society are innovative in their thinking.

If you have an idea that you believe will add value to peoples' lives, you should do whatever it takes to make it become a reality. There are people ready and willing to invest money in a good business idea. Someone believed in Bill Gates' vision for Microsoft and they received a wonderful return on their investment.

How can I earn more? If you are passionate about your idea and you believe in it, do your due diligence by writing a business plan. When your business plan is professionally completed, you can now market your business idea to potential investors. If you are finding it difficult to find adequate financing, you may want to consider finding another source of income to finance your own idea to make your dream a reality.

"I Am the Master of Money" This is the most sophisticated money language where leverage is power. This is when wealth building is the mindset and the lifestyle. Those who speak this money language know that their earning potential is unlimited. **They invest their**

time and money in the creators of society. We call this the mastery level of the language of money.

To reach the mastery level of money, one must have enough useable income to invest in other businesses or startups. These types of investment vehicles can exponentially increase your earning power, provided that you have done your due diligence in your choice of business investment. These investments will continue to yield income for you as long as the business is lucrative. If you desire to reach this level of money mastery, speak to someone who has demonstrated sound financial business investing in their life. When you do what wealthy people do, you create wealth. Wealthy people understand that abundance comes from enriching others. **Keep pressing forward with financial wisdom and surely you will be a wealth builder.**

ATTRACTIVE
BROWN
INTERIOR
ADULT
BEAUTIFUL
BALL
SHINY
IMAGE
AUTUMN
FEMALE
MAN
BROCHURE
MARKET
CONCEPT
BOW
HAPPY
PAPER
CREDIT
FUN
SUIT
ENTERTAINMENT
DRESSED
WEDDING
SUCCESS
RETRO
LIGHT
CASH
WEALTH
PORTRAIT
COLOR
POSTER
COVER
OLD
MAN
ABSTRACT
SYMBOL
GIRL
OBJECT
PEOPLE
GOLD
WOMAN
GIRL
GLAMOUR
DECORATION
RICH
HOLDING
PARTY
GLASS
COLOR
BRIGHT
BROWN
FINANCIAL
HANDSOME
INVESTMENT
WEALTH
CARD
SYMBOL
ELEGANT
GROWTH
BEAUTY
PARTY
LIFESTYLE
ANTIQUE
VINTAGE
FASHION
PATTERN
FEMALE
BOW
MARKET
RICH
FRAME
LUXURY
YOUNG
PLANT
ELEGANT
MALE
BUSINESS
PERSON
WALL
SOFA
PEOPLE
ART
FORMAL
FINANCE
TEMPLATE
BRUNETTE
LIFESTYLE
GLASS
BANKING
TABLE
SHINY
VINTAGE
PERSON
MONEY
GROWTH
DETAIL
DESIGN
CARD
BUSINESS
WOMAN
STYLE
BORDER
RETRO
MONEY
WELL
WEBSITE
SIGN
CAUCASIAN
DAY
METAL
ANTIQUE
FORMAL
SUIT
FRAME
FINANCE
CASH
TEXTURE
DECORATION
SOFA
BANK
OLD
SUCCESS
WEDDING
DESIGN
OBJECT
DRESS
WELL
LUXURY
BEAUTY
DRESS
IMAGE
FASHION
COMMERCIAL
COVER
BALL
TABLE
WEBSITE
CURRENCY
INVESTMENT

> *"I have about concluded that wealth is a state of mind, and that anyone can acquire a wealthy state of mind by thinking rich thoughts."* - *Andrew Young*

CHAPTER V
THE IMPLEMENTATION OF
WEALTH BUILDING STRATEGIES

Financial goals are like dreams. Wake up and face reality. We all have the right to pursue peace, happiness and the path of prosperity. You can enjoy the power of becoming financially independent, if you make a decision to invest wisely, have short-term and long-term financial goals, and circulate your cash with a purpose. In the game of finances there are rules. If you don't know them and you don't obey them, you won't succeed. The problem is that when it comes to wealth, most of us have never been taught the rules, and we don't know who to ask. The key is to find and learn from those who know and LIVE the rules. Fortunately for you, "the rules" of wealth are outlined in this book. No mind ever receives the truth until it is prepared to receive it.

There is a shocking truth about wealth: Wealth adores a person who has a healthy attitude towards it. **Thoughts of your mind have made you what you are, and the thoughts of your mind will make you whatever you become from this day forward**. You cannot change what you do not acknowledge. Get real with yourself about your life and your finances. Once you realize this, you will come to fully understand that people, places, conditions and events cannot keep wealth from coming to you. **In a financial war, most of the decisive battles are fought within YOU.**

You are accountable for your life. If you step up and take responsibility for your choices - not just your future choices, but all your past choices - you will begin to see clearly what financial habits you need to change.

"No one is in control of your happiness but you; therefore, you have the power to change anything about yourself or your life that you want to change." Barbara de Angelis PHD.

Today is the day you need to take action in regards to whatever financial situation you may be in. You have the power to eliminate all financial pressures and discover the joy of financial freedom. It begins with self-discipline and a vision. Begin to see yourself financially free, allow this to propel and motivate you into action. A positive attitude that arises from a firm belief that "you can succeed" is essential, but action is also mandatory.

Are you committed to being a wealth builder? This is not for the fainthearted. It will require discipline, focus and commitment. **To procrastinate is to commit to do nothing**. What you intend to do doesn't matter. What matters is what you actually do. **Your excuses won't feed your family.** Don't accept your own excuses. Your family and friend don't need them and your critics won't believe them.

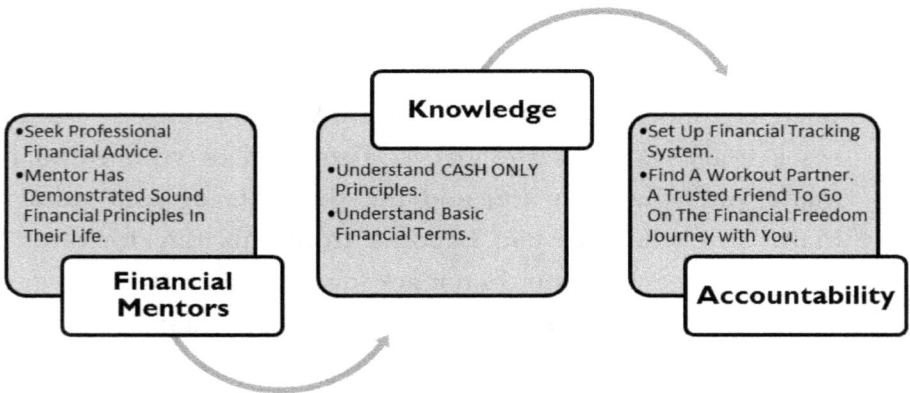

Knowledge

- Understand CASH ONLY Principles.
- Understand Basic Financial Terms.

Financial Mentors

- Seek Professional Financial Advice.
- Mentor Has Demonstrated Sound Financial Principles In Their Life.

Accountability

- Set Up Financial Tracking System.
- Find A Workout Partner. A Trusted Friend To Go On The Financial Freedom Journey with You.

Got a Financial Plan?

Many people get nervous when they hear the word "financial plan" because they do not have a full understanding of it. Having a plan for your finances is the most important thing you can do to help you be financially successful. A financial plan is more than being able to pay your bills on time. The basic idea behind financial planning is to save and invest money with a purpose. Studies show that simply writing down a plan increases your chance of success by more than 30%.

I have heard people whine about being too busy with their daily routine to create a financial plan. All they want to do is go to work, pay their monthly bills, and have a few dollars to go drinking on the weekend. Some people will try to run from the truth until their backs are against the wall and they have to face the music. Change is scary for some people.

Sometime in the past, these individuals stopped playing to win and started playing not to lose and now they are losing big time. Fear of failure, peer pressure and discomfort at the thought of leaving their routine lulled them to settle instead of going for what they truly desire. They would rather spend 8 to 10 hours on a job they do not like and then come home and spend 4 hours in front of the idiot box (TV) in an attempt to escape their mental prison.

The more knowledge you have about the bad habits you want to overcome, the more successful you will be in conquering them. Many people would live a wonderful life if they knew how to manage their money and track their expenses. There are many people who make a great deal of money but are broke because they do not manage their money well. With a financial plan, you have the tools to decide exactly what is going to happen with your earned income.

Recognize that you have all the tools necessary to accomplish what you want financially. You must become good at planning and each and every day, you must work your financial plan by setting priorities to accomplish your financial goals. It is extremely important to know how much money you have to circulate, to invest and to save. Seek counsel from someone who has demonstrated sound financial discipline in their life. **"Never take advice from anyone more screwed up than you are."** - John Addison.

It is important to your financial future that you know you are headed in the right financial direction. If you are completely honest with yourself, a financial plan is the guide to let you know if you are on track to accomplish your financial goals.

It does not matter how much money you make, it is how much you keep that counts. If you do not learn and develop the financial habits that would make your money work for you, you will never have enough money. Take charge of your finances and become a master of money. To get to the level of having financial freedom, you must take control of your finances, and it requires the right financial habits.

You can be in control of your money instead of letting it control you. Remember that no one will care more about your financial future than you. Begin to create a plan of action today that will convert your financial dreams into reality. You may want to start subscribing to financial publications such as Forbes, Money or Fortune. Also choose to read the Wall Street Journal instead of the trash news.

History is often written by people who believe in a dream so intensely that they are willing to commit themselves totally to the realization of that dream. You have probably heard it said before that it is impossible to succeed without believing. In other words, if you want to succeed in life, then you must believe in what you are doing. It is called faith and with it, your possibilities in life are limitless. Without faith, the complete opposite is true and leads you down a pathway of failure every time.

If you want to live a successful life, free from the worry of debt and constantly focusing on how you are going to pay your bills, then eliminate doubt of any kind from your life. Doubt is the opposite of faith and it is the number one destroyer of success. Do not allow doubt to creep into your life and ruin what God has in store for you. Be proactive and use your faith and belief to stop doubt in its track. Use your faith to drive you toward success. The situations and circumstances around you must change because of your faith.

"Faith is to believe what you do not see; the reward of this faith is to see what you believe." **St. Augustine**

Being wise with your money is a process, step by step not a one-time all or nothing dash for the cash. As you make a firm decision to become financially free, you must have a builder's mentality and a blueprint for your financial goals. You do not have to take unnecessary risks to be financially successful. Once you have a plan of action to earn your first million, acquiring the second million is much easier. To broaden your financial thoughts, T. Boone Picken stated: *"The First Billion is the Hardest."* The difference between those who achieved true financial success and those who continue to struggle, no matter how much money is coming into their home, is based on the possession of a wealthy mindset. Wealthy people have a dream that they are committed to, and they continue to work at it until it becomes a reality.

Have you paid yourself today? Do you save 20% of everything you earn? I do not believe it to be sensible to work a full week and as soon as you receive your check, you give it all away to pay bills. You need to develop the habit of paying yourself first. Every time you are paid for services rendered, make sure you keep a portion of that income to save and invest for you and your family.

Declare: A portion of my income is mine to keep to save and invest in my financial freedom.

We who have worked to achieved financial success, believe and know we deserve to keep a portion of all we earn. We are unwilling to rely on others or circumstances to determine our financial future. We have an understanding of the financial principles, obtain assets and create the circumstances for our own success. We make things happen rather than simply waiting for something to happen.

When you pay your bills, the first check you must write is to yourself. Always pay yourself first – prior to spending any money, make that sacrifice to pay yourself first and from this, you should put away some in an investment plan and also your savings. Consider yourself as a bill to yourself; pay that bill and deposit that money in your financial freedom account. Pay yourself first even if you believe you cannot afford it. The truth is, you cannot afford not to. Pay that money to yourself even if you have to cut that cable bill. The time you spend mesmerized by someone else's life on television you can be using to create the magnificent new life that will make others stand in awe. Be Wealthy! Go ahead; I dare you!

How to Accomplish More in Less Time

As the saying goes, "time is money." And in fact, oftentimes, time is actually more important than money. You can certainly make use of time intelligently to make back money you've lost but even if you have the wealth of Bill Gates, a second lost is a second lost. There is simply no way you can buy back lost time. **Time will either promote you or expose you.**

This brings us to the topic of the importance of knowing how to maximize the use of our time. Don't we all wish we could maximize the effectiveness of every minute in the working day? In order to do that, it is critically important to identify the time-wasting habits in our lives—those little seemingly harmless activities that are actually sucking time from us without our knowledge. These are the activities that cause you to wonder at the end of the day, "Where has all my time gone?"

Time is your most precious resource. Utilizing your time effectively to accomplish your financial goals is actually not as difficult as it seems and all it requires is a reorganization of your thoughts and the way you handle and plan out your daily activities.

First and foremost, you need a "Get It Done" list. Having a "Get It Done" list instead of a "To Do" list gives you a sense of direction and lets you know exactly what it is you are supposed to get done for that day. A "Get It Done" list should only have 3 to 5 "important" things that must get done. I like to call it my 3 to 5 income-producing activities, and mowing the lawn is not one of them. You have to determine what's important to you and "Get It Done."

Secondly, you need to get into the habit of splitting your time into manageable blocks that you can handle. The size of your time blocks would depend on the nature of your activities. You would split them into fifteen minutes, half an hour or one-hour blocks depending on your needs. Tie this in with your "Get It Done" list and allocate chunks of your time to each activity to your list.

Lastly, and perhaps most importantly, take action! A "Get It Done" list is not to be made to be "looked at" it is made to be acted on. Your family, business and finances don't care about your intentions. They care about what you do. If you are known to procrastinate, find yourself an accountability partner.

Utilize your "Get It Done" list for the next 30 days, and I am sure you will gain so much insight into where all your time goes that you will get addicted to it. **Productivity produces income.** Determine how much time you spend on productive activities and how much time you spend on tedious work.

Learn and take action. It really does not matter where you were or where you are now; it matters where you are going. Our desire is for you to begin setting financial goals to achieve results. These goals may be either short- or long-term. Long-term goals can take about three to five years to achieve, while short-term goals are attainable within six months to three years. Short-term goals are often a stop along the way to your long term goals.

The right way to set and achieve your financial goals: S.M.A.R.T.

People routinely make resolutions about accomplishing major goals: earning more money, getting a promotion, losing weight, building better relationships – and then fail to fulfill them. Resolutions don't work. What works is creating new habits that lead to the results you want for the rest of your life. However, some people do keep their commitment to themselves and achieve their goals. They succeed because they set demanding goals that motivate, challenge and inspire them.

Specific. Your goals must be desirable, something you want to accomplish. This is the Who? What? When? and Why?

Set specific goals. Most people have goals to be successful, get rich, improve relationships and the like, but these are very vague and the mind can become confused. If we can imagine something, see it or picture it, we're a lot more likely to process, understand and embrace it. Visualize your goals. The better you are able to do this the easier it is for your subconscious to embrace your goals. Specific goals like "I will earn $500,000 by the end of this year," or "I will become the sales manager of the sales division by next month," or "I will invest in my marriage, my spouse and I will attend a marriage retreat twice a year." are much more effective and allow you to measure your progress. Include the amount, position name, and the date and all the important details needed to train your mind to start working towards that goal. If you want results that you can be proud of, be specific.

Measurable. What am I doing to track my progress?

Goals need to be measurable so that you can gauge how well you are doing. To help measure your paths and goals, you should include measurable details. For your job, you can include details such as the number of hours you are working, the amount you are earning, the staff you are handling, etc. For your financial goals, you can include details such as the amount you want to have as a whole or the amount you want to earn on a monthly basis. Always have important points and items to be measured so you can understand how close you are to achieving your goals. If your goal is to earn $50,000 a month, then you know you are halfway there if you're already earning $25,000 a month. But how do you get to $50,000 a month?

Attainable. Your goals must be achievable.

In the beginning stages of setting goals, some people set goals that are so high to reach that they are almost setting up things that may be challenging to achieve. It is ok to set challenging goals, just make sure you set objectives that you can reach within a given amount of time, provided the current resources and capabilities you have. Some goals can be achieved faster compared to others if you have the knowledge and skills to pursue them. When you list your goals, and start devising a plan to reach them, goals become more attainable because you are focused. Each day, ask yourself, "What must I accomplish today in order to know that I'm on track to achieve my goals?"

Realistic. Your goals must be believable to YOU!

Goals should be challenging, but also realistic. The best way to set goals is to set a parameter outside of your comfort zone – but not so far outside that it seems wildly impossible. Goal-setting should be aspirational so do not be afraid to think big and reach for your goals. At the same time, make sure you are empowered and equipped to achieve your goals. Such ambitious goals probably will make you feel fearful at some point. Be prepared to deal with these emotions. Your plans and goals can be destroyed by fear. Take the time to identify and understand your fears. An excellent way to overcome fear is by taking action. Fear disappears once you start to do something that is productive.

Time. Your goals must have a timetable, a specific time frame to reach your goal. **Time will either promote you or expose you.**

You must feel a sense of urgency about your goals or they will never happen. Setting the exact time and date will spur you to start working on your goals instead of putting it off for another day. Some goals can take years to accomplish so it is wiser to break these down into smaller objectives. Each day, ask yourself, "What did I do today to advance my goals?"

The key is: You must act on your goals every day. For the next 30 days, review the financial goals you have set for yourself. Review your goals every morning, throughout the day, and during the evening. Force your goals into your subconscious mind; see yourself as already having attained them. Like repetition, visualization is a technique you can use to get what you want. Do this consistently every day for the next 30 days and it will become a habit. A habit that will lead you from one success to another all the days of your life.

"Good habits are the key to all success. Bad habits are the unlocked door to failure. I will form good habits and become their slaves." **Og Mandino**

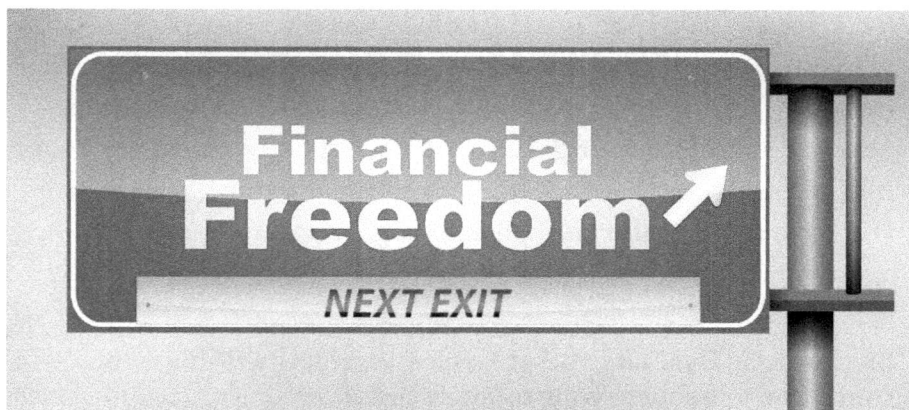

7 Steps to Financial Freedom

Here is a seven-step goal-setting exercise that you can use to set and achieve your financial goals. These action steps summarize the best techniques for setting goals and streamlining your activities, enabling you to accomplish vastly more than the average person.

Step No. 1: Know your financial freedom number.

You need to know exactly what amount you will need coming in, passively on a monthly basis, that would give you financial freedom. Write down a specific dollar amount that you feel you will need to live a comfortable life. This is for you and your family; you do not need anyone's approval about how small or large this number should be.

Financial planning and goal-setting are long-term commitments we make to ourselves and our family. A good way to start is to identify both your short-term and long-term goals. If your financial freedom number is $500,000 per year, then stick with it and do not deviate from it.

Step No. 2: Have a reason why and know how it would make you feel to achieve your financial goal.

Your reason: **Why?** must be much bigger than just paying your bills. Your "why" must motivate you, because you must become more to earn more. It will be a process you must go through before you achieve your goal. If you have the expectation to be a millionaire, know that it is going to take some time, especially if you have never made more than $100,000 dollars in a given year or month.

Step No. 3: Evaluate the obstacles that you will have to overcome to achieve your financial goal.

Once you decide to be free, take consistent and persistent action. There will be obstacles you will need to overcome. For example, if you are a compulsive spender, you may need to stay away from the local shopping malls until you overcome your spending habits. Eliminate any self-defeating obstacles that will hinder you from achieving your goal. Stick to your commitment.

Step No. 4: You will need the proper tools that will empower you to have the skills needed to reach your financial goal.

In order to achieve a financial goal that you have never reached before, you must develop the knowledge and necessary skills needed to accomplish that financial goal. Jim Rohn, America's foremost business philosopher, said: *"After you become a millionaire, you can give all of your money away because what's important is not the million dollars; what's important is the person you have become in the process of becoming a millionaire."*

Every new goal requires that you become a new person, in some way, by developing additional knowledge and skills in order both to achieve it and to maintain it.

Step No. 5: Evaluate your associations. The people you surround yourself with will determine if you achieve your financial goal.

Achieving financial freedom requires the active cooperation of many people. Remember, it is all about relationships. Seek out those who have already achieved financial freedom. Do not be afraid to ask for help, even if it is in the form of advice and introductions from the people you know.

One person, one contact, can make all the difference between success and failure. Avoid negativity, including negative individuals who want to bring you down. Such people work against your best interests.

Step No. 6: Create a plan to achieve your financial goal.

Put your plan in writing and review it daily. Your plan becomes your compass to keep you on track. Make a list of your financial obligations. Organize the list into a plan based on priority and sequence. Everyone's financial freedom goal might be slightly different. Some might be content with their finances but are failing to plan for their children's college education or to put aside for their 401k or retirement. Whatever your inner voice is telling you to improve on is what needs to drive your passion.

Step No. 7: Take Action!

Once you begin, never stop. Do something every day that moves you toward the achievement of your financial goal. Develop a bias for action and a sense of urgency. Be persistent and consistent moving towards your goal.

Do whatever is necessary once you begin working on your goal; never stop until you achieve it. Get the results you desire. To accelerate the process of achieving your financial goal, create a clear mental picture of what your goal would look like as if you had already achieved it. Begin with the end in mind.

Visualize and imagine your goal as a reality. Imagine the feeling of joy and satisfaction you would feel when the goal is accomplished. Repeat over and over to yourself that you will achieve it. Never doubt for a minute that you will be triumphant.

Most importantly, journal your experience to achieving financial freedom. Then you will have a blueprint for others to follow. This will change your family's legacy.

Throughout history, the world's most successful people have used techniques like these to get what they want. These methods will work for you, regardless of your circumstances or what you may be up against. Your main job is to be absolutely clear about what it is you want, make a plan to achieve that goal, and then to think about it and work on it every single day. Remember, there are no limits except the limits you place on your own imagination. Wealth building is a process, enjoy the journey!

Master These Wealth Building Skills

- Get in the habit of paying yourself first

- Save 20% of all income

- Begin paying for things with CASH ONLY

- Learn to how to read a financial statement

- Accumulate assets, not liabilities

- Learn to protect your assets

- Study the global financial markets

- Put yourself in the position to have interest work in your favor and not against you. Be the lender, not the borrower

- Have your money work for you bringing in more money Money-Making Money!!!

FINANCIAL TERMS

Here is a list of commonly used terms and their definitions in the investment and financial industries:

A

Accounts Payable — Money a company owes for services and supplies. For example, a record company would list as accounts payable the bill from a wax company that supplied the raw material for making records.

Accrued Interest — The interest due on a bond since the last interest payment was made. The buyer of the bond pays the market price plus accrued interest.

Acquisition — Acquiring control of one corporation by another. In "unfriendly" takeover attempts, the potential buying company may offer a price well above current market values, new securities and other inducements to stockholders. The management of the subject company might ask for a better price or try to join up with a third company.

ADR — American Depositary Receipt. A security issued by a U.S. bank in place of the Foreign shares held in trust by that bank, thereby facilitating the trading of foreign shares in U.S. markets.

After Tax Return — The yield of an investment after taxes have been taken out.

American Stock Exchange — The second largest stock exchange in New York located in the financial district of New York City.

Amortization — Accounting for expenses or charges as applicable rather than as paid. Includes such practices as depreciation, depletion, write-off of intangibles, prepaid expenses and deferred charges.

Annual Report — The formal financial statement issued yearly by a publicly-owned corporation. The report shows assets, liabilities, revenues, expenses and earnings. The report also shows the company's financial condition at the close of the business year and other basic information of interest to shareholders.

Annuity — An individual pays an insurance company a specified capital sum in exchange for a promise that the insurer will, at some time in the future, begin to make a series of periodic payments to the individual for as long as he/she lives or for some other specified period of time.

Appreciation — An increase in fair market value.

Asset — Anything a person, company, or group owns or is owed, including money, investments and property.

B
Balance Sheet — A condensed financial statement showing the nature and amount of a company's assets, liabilities and capital on a given date. In dollar amounts, the balance sheet shows what the company owned, what it owed and the ownership interest in the company of its stockholders.

Basis Point — One gradation on a 100-point scale representing one percent; used especially in expressing variations in the yields of bonds. Fixed income yields vary often and slightly within one percent, and the basis point scale easily expresses these changes in hundredths of one percent.

Bear — Someone who believes the market will decline.

Bear Market — A condition of the stock market when prices of stocks are generally declining.

Beneficiary — One who is designated to receive a benefit. Example: person who would receive the proceeds of a life insurance settlement.

Bid and Asked — The "bid" is the highest price anyone is willing to pay for a security at a given time; the "asked" is the lowest price anyone will take at that time. Stocks are usually purchased at "bid" and sold at "asked."

Blue-Chip Stock — Stock in a company with a national reputation for quality, reliability and the ability to operate profitably in good and bad times.

Bond — A promise of a corporation, municipality, government, church and the like, to pay interest at a stated rate and repay face value of the bond which is actually a loan from you to the corporation or other entity at a specified maturity date.

Borrowing — A way of acquiring necessary capital. One form of borrowing is when an individual or a company asks a bank to loan them a certain amount of money over a certain period of time, and agrees to pay a certain amount of interest.

Broker — An agent who handles the public's orders to buy and sell securities, commodities or other property. For this service, a commission is charged.

Budget — A plan or guideline for spending.

Bull — One who believes the market will rise.

Bull Market — A condition of the stock market when prices of stocks are generally rising.

C

Capital Gain — Profit made on securities, either through dividends or by selling the securities for a higher price than they originally cost.

Capitalization — Total amount of various securities issued by a corporation. Capitalization may include bonds, debentures, preferred and common stock, and surplus.

Capital Needs — In personal financial planning, the amount of capital (assets or cash) needed in a lump sum to enable one to meet income needs and expenses should death or disability occur.

Cash Flow — The process of money coming in from various sources (income) and being spent on various uses (expenses). A cash flow statement is a look at both the income and the expenses over any period of time, but it is usually for at least a month and/or a year.

Certificate — The actual piece of paper that is evidence of ownership of stock in a corporation. Watermarked paper is finely engraved with delicate etchings to discourage forgery.

Certificate of Deposit (CD) — An agreement with a bank that you will leave your money on deposit for a specified period of time in return for a specific amount of interest.

Collateral — Securities or other property pledged by a borrower to secure repayment of a loan.

Commercial Paper — Debt instruments issued by companies to meet short-term financing needs.

Commission — The broker's basic fee for purchasing or selling securities or property as an agent.

Common Stock — Securities that represent an ownership interest in a corporation. They generally have dividend and appreciation potential.

Corporate Bond — A bond issued by a corporation.

Current Assets — Those assets that can easily be converted into cash or sold in a short period of time. Example: stocks, certificates of deposit, cash value of life insurance and money market funds; also known as liquid assets.

Current Liabilities — Money owed and payable by a company, usually within one year.

D
Day Order — An order to buy or sell which, if not executed, expires at the end of the trading day on which it was entered.

Debt — A sum owed to someone else, either a financial or personal obligation; a state of owing.

Debit Balance — In a customer's margin account, that portion of the purchase price of stock, bonds or commodities that is covered by credit extended by the broker to the margin customer.

Depreciation — Normally charges against earnings to write off the cost, less salvage value, of an asset over its estimated useful life. It is a bookkeeping entry and does not represent any cash outlay, nor are funds earmarked for the purpose.

Discretionary Account — An account in which the customer gives the broker or someone else discretion to buy and sell securities or commodities including selection, timing, amount and price to be paid or received.

Diversification — Spreading money among different types of investments.

Dividend — The payment designated by a corporation to be distributed pro rata among outstanding shares of stock. Corporations usually declare dividends from their profits, and the amount is in relation to the amount of the profit.

Dividend Election — The method in which you choose to receive your dividends. Most commonly refers to life insurance. You may elect dividends to be paid in cash, to reduce premiums, to buy paid-up additions, or to accumulate at interest.

Dollar Cost Averaging — A method of purchasing securities at regular intervals with a fixed amount of dollars regardless of the prevailing prices of the securities. Payments buy more shares when the price is low and fewer shares when it rises.

E
Earnings Report — A statement – also called an income statement – issued by a company, showing its earnings or losses over a given period. The earnings report lists the income earned, expenses and the net result.

Economic Indicator — A key statistic in the overall economy that experts use as a yardstick to predict the performance of the stock market.

Effective Rate — The amount of each dollar earned that goes to pay taxes. The ratio of total taxes paid to gross income.

Equity — The ownership interest of common and preferred stockholders in a company.

Exercise — Action taken by an option holder that requires the writer to perform the terms of the contract.

Exercise Prices — The prices at which an option may be exercised. Also called strike prices.

Expiration Date — The date the option contract expires.

F
Face Value — The value of a bond that appears on the face of the bond unless the value is otherwise specified by the issuing company. Face value is ordinarily the amount the issuing company promises to pay at maturity. Face value is not an indication of market value.

Fair Market Price — A reasonable price for securities based on supply and demand.

Fiduciary — One who acts for another in financial matters.

Financial Futures — Futures contracts based on financial instruments such as U.S. Treasury bonds, CDs and other interest-sensitive issues, currencies and stock market indicators.

Fiscal Year — A corporation's accounting year. Due to the nature of that particular business, some companies do not use the calendar year for their bookkeeping.

Floor — The huge trading area where stocks are bought and sold on the New York Stock Exchange (NYSE).

Floor Brokers — The largest single membership group of the NYSE. There are two main types: Commission brokers, employed by brokerage houses, buy and sell securities on the NYSE floor for the general public. Independent floor brokers work for themselves. They execute orders for brokerages without full-time commission brokers or for overly busy brokers.

Free and Open Market — A market in which supply and demand are freely expressed in terms of price. Contrasts with a controlled market in which supply, demand and price may all be regulated.

Fundamental Research — Analysis of industries and companies based on such factors as sales, assets, earnings, products or services, markets and management. As applied to the economy, fundamental research includes consideration of gross national product, interest rates, unemployment, inventories, savings, etc.

Futures — A contract specifying a future date of delivery or receipt of a certain amount of a specific tangible or intangible product. The commodities traded in futures markets include stock index futures; agricultural products like wheat, soybeans and pork bellies; metals; and financial instruments.

G
Good 'Til Canceled (GTC) — An order to buy or sell at a specific price until the investor cancels the order.

Going Public — When a company sells shares of itself to the public to raise capital.

Government Bond — A bond issued by the federal government.

Growth Stock — Stock of a company with a record of earnings growth at a relatively high rate.

H
Hedging — The purchase or sale of a derivative security (such as options or futures) in order to reduce or neutralize all or some portion of the risk of holding another security.

Holding Company — A corporation that owns the securities of another, in most cases with voting control.

I
Income Statement — A report on a company's financial status over a period of time. It totals profits, subtracts expenses and pinpoints how much money the company can reinvest.

Income Stock — Common stocks that pay large dividends that an investor could use as income.

Index — A statistical yardstick expressed in terms of percentages of a base year or years. For instance, the NYSE Composite Index of all NYSE common stocks is based on year-end 1965 as 50. An index is not an average.

Individual Retirement Account (IRA) — A retirement provision established by law that allows an individual to deduct from his income a certain amount set aside for future retirement.

Inflation —— An increase in the volume of money and credit relative to available goods resulting in a substantial and continuing rise in the general price level.

Inflation Rate — An important economic indicator; the rate at which prices are rising.

Initial Public Offering (IPO) — A corporation's first offering of stock to the public.

Investment - The use of money for the purpose of making more money: to gain income, increase capital, save taxes, or a combination of the three.

Investment Portfolio — A variety of securities owned by an individual or an institution.

Issue — Any of a company's securities, or the act of distributing such securities.

K
Keogh Plan — Tax advantaged personal retirement program that can be established by a self-employed individual.

L
Liabilities — All the claims against a corporation. Liabilities include accounts, wages and salaries payable; dividends declared payable; accrued taxes payable; fixed or long-term liabilities, such as mortgage bonds, debentures and bank loans. (see Assets, Balance Sheet)

Limit Order — An order to buy or sell when and if a security reaches a specific price.

Liquidate — When a company fails, the process of converting all of its assets back into cash and distributing it to those with a claim on it.

Liquidity — How easily one's assets can be converted back into cash. Liquidity is one of the most important characteristics of a good market.

Long-Term Assets — Those assets that cannot easily be converted to cash or sold or consumed in a short period of time. Example: home, real estate and land assets.

M

Margin — The amount paid by the customer when using a broker's credit to buy or sell a security. Under Federal Reserve regulations, the initial margin required since 1934 has ranged from 40% of the purchase price up to 100%. Since 1974, the current rate of 50% has been in effect.

Market Order — An order to buy or sell at the best price currently available on the Trading Floor.

Market Price — The last reported price at which the stock or bond sold, or the current quote.

Maturity Date — The date that a bond comes due and must be paid off.

Merger — A combination of two or more corporations.

Minimum Deposit — When the cash value increases in the insurance policy and is used to pay the premiums of the policy.

Mortgage — Usually refers to the balance of the loan on a home. The amount of money borrowed to purchase a home.

Money Market Account — An account in which your money is reinvested in short-term securities by the bank or investment firm managing the account.

Money Market Fund — A mutual fund whose investments are in high-yield money market instruments such as federal securities, CDs and commercial paper. Its intent is to make such instruments, normally purchased in large denominations by institutions, available indirectly to individuals.

Mortgage Bond — A bond secured by a mortgage on a property. The value of the property may or may not equal the value of the bond issued against it.

Municipal Bond — A bond issued by a county, city, district or authority.

N

NASD — The National Association of Securities Dealers, an association of brokers and dealers in the over-the-counter securities business.

Nasdaq — commonly known as the NASDAQ, is an American stock exchange. It is the second-largest exchange in the world by market capitalization, behind only the New York Stock Exchange.

Non-Liquid — Investments not easily converted to cash at their current fair market value.

O

Offer — The price at which a person is ready to sell. Opposed to bid, the price at which one is ready to buy.

Options — A right to buy or sell a fixed amount of a given stock at a specified price within a limited period of time. If the right is not exercised, the option expires and the buyer forfeits the money.

Orders — Specific instructions for handling transactions.

Over-The-Counter (OTC) — A market for securities made up of dealers who may or may not be members of a securities exchange. The OTC market is conducted over the telephone and deals mainly with stocks of companies without sufficient shares, stockholders or earnings to warrant listing on an exchange.

P

Par — Equal to the nominal or face value of a security.

Preferred Stock — Similar to common stock. Generally, less dividend and appreciation potential but receives a higher priority or preference over common stock in dividend payments or in the event of liquidation.

Premium — The payment an insurance policy holder agrees to make for coverage.

Present Value — The value of a sum of money to be received in the future in today's dollars, taking into account either interest rates, inflation or both.

Prime Rate — The interest rate charged by large U.S. money center commercial banks to their best business borrowers.

Principle — A person's capital or money which is used for investments. Sometimes referred to as equity when talking about a house.

Prospectus — A circular that describes securities or investments being offered for sale to the public.

Proxy — Written authorization given by a shareholder to someone else to represent him and vote his shares at a shareholder's meeting.

Proxy Statement — Information given to stockholders in conjunction with the solicitation of proxies.

Purchasing Power - The ability of a dollar to buy a product or service. As prices increase, purchasing power decreases.

Q

Quote — The highest bid to buy and the lowest offer to sell any stock at a given time.

R

Rate of Return — In stocks and bonds, the amount of money returned to investors on their investments. Also known as yield.

Recession — A period of no or negative economic growth and high unemployment.

Refinancing — Same as refunding. New securities are sold by a company and the money is used to retire existing securities. Objective may be to save interest costs, extend the maturity of the loan or both.

Reinvest — Funneling of profits back into a company to enhance its operations. An individual stockowner can also reinvest by designating that dividends paid on stock will be used to purchase additional shares of that stock.

REIT — A Real Estate Investment Trust is an organization similar to an investment company in some respects but concentrating its holdings in real estate investments. The yield is generally liberal since REITs are required to distribute as much as 90% of their income.

Retained Earnings — Profits a company keeps for its operations after paying taxes and dividends.

Right to vote — The right of common stockholders to vote on matters of corporate policy at an annual stockholder's meeting.

S

Securities and Exchange Commission (SEC) — The Securities and Exchange Commission established by Congress to help protect investors, monitor the securities industry and enforce punishments on those that violate the industry's regulations. The SEC administers the Securities Act of 1933, the Securities Exchange Act of 1934, the Securities Act Amendment of 1975, the Trust Indenture Act, the Investment Company Act, the Investment Advisers Act, and the Public Utility Holding Company Act.

Securities Investors Protection Corporation (SIPC) — A safeguard for investors capital created by Congress. The SIPC insures that cash and securities on deposit with a brokerage are insured up to $500,000 per customer in the event that the brokerage goes out of business.

Stockholders' Equity — The value of all the stock owned by the shareholders of a particular company. Also known as net worth.

Syndicate — A group of investment bankers who, together, underwrite and distribute a new issue of securities or a large block of an outstanding issue.

T

Ticker — A telegraphic system that continuously provides the last sale prices and volume of securities transactions on exchanges. Information is either printed or displayed on a moving tape after each trade.

Treasuries — Debt obligations of the U.S. government. Treasuries are among the safest investments since they are secured by the full faith and credit of the government. The interest of Treasuries is exempt from state and local taxes but is subject to federal income tax. There are three types of treasuries: Treasury Bills with maturities of 1 year or less; Treasury Notes with maturities ranging from 1 to 10 years; and Treasury Bonds which are long-term instruments with maturities of 10 years or more.

Treasury Stock — Stock issued by a company but later reacquired. It may be held in the company's treasury indefinitely, reissued to the public or retired. Treasury stock receives no dividend and has no vote while held by the company.

U

Unlisted Stock — A security not listed on a stock exchange.

V

Variable Annuity — A life insurance policy where the annuity premium (a set amount of dollars) is immediately turned into units of a portfolio of stock. Upon retirement, the policyholder is paid accordingly to accumulated units, the dollar value of which varies according to the performance of the stock portfolio. Its objective is to enhance, through stock investment, the purchasing value of the annuity which otherwise is subject to erosion through inflation.

W

Will — The directions of a testator (the person who makes a will) regarding the final disposition of his or her estate.

Withholding — Refers to the amount of tax withheld from a paycheck.

Working Capital — The assets a company has that can be invested into the company's operations.

Y

Yield — In stocks and bonds, the amount of money returned to investors on their investments. Also known as rate of return.

Yield to Maturity — The yield of a bond to maturity takes into account the price discount from or premium over the face amount. It is greater than the current yield when the bond is selling at a discount and less than the current yield when the bond is selling at a premium.

Z

Zero Coupon Bond — A bond which pays no interest but at issue, is priced at a discount from its redemption price.

BIBLIOGRAPHY

All Scriptures are from the King James Version unless otherwise noted.

Francis, Hasheem, and Francis, Deborah, **Built To Prosper The Principles of Developing Your Greatest Asset; YOU** Plymouth, FL.: Loyal Leaders Publishing, 2010.

Baines, John. **The Secret Science**.: John Baines Institute, 1994.

Francis, Deborah **The Joy of Healthy Living, Without Your Health You Cannot Enjoy Your Wealth**. Plymouth, FL.: The Joy of Healthy Living, LLC, 2011.

Generation Broke: Growth of Debt Among Young Americans http:// www.consolidatedcredit.org.

Haanel, Charles. F. **The Master Key System**. St. Louis: Psychology Publishing, 1916.

Hill, Napoleon **Think and Grow Rich**. New York, NY: Penguin, 2008.

Thompson, Leroy, Dr. **Money Cometh: To The Body of Christ**. Darrow, LA: Ever Increasing Word Ministries, 1999.

Thompson, Leroy, Dr. **I'll Never Be Broke Another Day in My Life**. Darrow, LA: Ever Increasing Word Ministries, 2001.

Wattles, Wallace. D. **The Science Of Getting Rich**. New York: Elizabeth Towne Company, 1910.

Wattles, Wallace. D. **The Science Of Being Well**. New York: Elizabeth Towne Company, 1910.

Investopedia: http://www.investopedia.com.

Hasheem Francis is the Chairman and CEO of Built To Prosper Companies. Hasheem is an entrepreneur, investor, best-selling author, keynote speaker, recognized industry thought leader, and an expert on executive business and leadership development. With two decades of entrepreneurial and leadership experience, Hasheem is a leadership consultant and advisor to CEOs, business leaders, corporate executives, and community leaders across the country.

Deborah Francis is the COO and President of Built To Prosper Companies. Deborah is an entrepreneur, best-selling author, investor, keynote speaker, recognized industry thought leader, and an expert on business development. Deborah has developed curriculums and delivered training sessions on entrepreneurship, small business development, and professional development. Deborah has trained, led and mentored hundreds of people with her functional knowledge and educational background. Deborah has a Masters in Secondary Education of English.

Books by Hasheem Francis & Deborah Francis:

Built To Prosper
Built To Prosper For Women
Built To Prosper For Financially
Built To Prosper Women of Wisdom Journal
Built To Prosper Wealth of Wisdom Journal
The Joy of Healthy Living; The Guide To Eating Right For Life
Cashology The Science of Living A Cash Only Life
Cashology Academy Wealth Workbook
Cashology Academy Wealth Journal
Undeniable Confidence
The Power of Effective Communication
The Science of Getting Rich: The Key To Peace, Power, & Prosperity

Built To Prosper Companies is an innovative business network that provides strategic consulting in a diverse portfolio of companies. As a leading provider of business consulting and training since 1999, **Built To Prosper Companies** has worked with over 1500 small to medium sized businesses.

Built To Prosper Companies specializes in business: planning, marketing, leadership development, and organizational sales training. We equip entrepreneurs, senior leaders and business advisors across 110 countries with the insights and actionable solutions they need to respond quickly to evolving business conditions and transform operations.

As the leading provider of consulting and training in the business services industry, **Built To Prosper Companies** produces value and unparalleled results for companies by delivering business solutions that support them in driving revenue growth. This is done with an uncompromising commitment toward serving our clients with the utmost respect, integrity, and the highest standards of excellence. Our delivery model is predicated on exacting alignment with the unique aspects of each client's business strategy, organizational structure and culture, ensuring each client engagement provides clear and actionable tactics that will drive success on an ongoing, quantifiable basis.

We believe that by delivering on this promise, we will help our clients not only drive incremental revenue growth, but also bring more meaning and fulfillment to our clients, their business, and the clients they serve.

Built To Prosper Companies is headquartered in Orlando, FL, with affiliate operations in New York, NY, and Hilton Head, SC.

Visit us: www.BuiltToProsperCompanies.com

BUILT TO PROSPER
SEMINARS
INTERNATIONAL PROFESSIONAL SPEAKERS

BUILT TO PROSPER SEMINARS will give you proven strategies to sharpen your leadership skills, business skills, financial and investment knowledge, relationships, spiritual life, and enjoy a healthy lifestyle.

Trainings & Seminars By Built To Prosper Seminars

Built To Prosper U
Cashology Academy
Loyal Leaders Seminar
The Joy Of Healthy Living
Young Entrepreneur's Academy
Emerging Business Boot Camp

We have a team who specialize in taking care of all our events and making sure we fully understand your needs as an organization. We have been producing amazing results for our clients and seminar participants for over a decade.

If you are interested in bringing Built To Prosper Seminars to your city, please send all request to: info@BTPCompanies.com.

BUILT TO PROSPER
—————MENTORING—————
BUSINESS AND LEADERSHIP DEVELOPMENT

Built To Prosper Mentoring® **Programs** are designed to empower you with the training, focus and accountability you need to achieve the consistent results you demand in the most important areas of your life. In order to succeed at the game of life, you must take action. We promise an experience that will not only stretch you but will be more fun than you have ever imagined possible. It is time you get results in your life.

Our programs are designed to address specific areas of personal and professional development.

Visit us: www.BTPMentoring.com

BTP
Publishing Group
WHERE LEADERS HAVE A VOICE

BTP Publishing Group is a pioneer in inventory book publishing, printing, fulfillment and distribution. We continue to expand our inventory book fulfillment network, allowing publishers and authors to seamlessly distribute their content through existing channels, as well as to leading retailers, e-tailers, distributors and other specialty book sale markets.

BTP Publishing Group provides professional services that enable authors to publish their own work and by doing so, allows authors to retain control of their book's sales strategies and profits.

Our Services
Offering a wide range of services from professional book interior and exterior design to editing and promotional tools, thousands of authors have taken advantage of our Unique Publishing System platform and expert staff to make their dreams a reality.

For more information visit: www.BTPPublish.com